A BASIC GUIDE TO READING INSTRUCTION

A Handbook for Classroom Teachers

Robert C. Putt
Mansfield University

Illustrated by
Deb Putt Payne

UNIVERSITY
PRESS OF
AMERICA

LANHAM • NEW YORK • LONDON

Copyright © 1983 by

University Press of America,™ Inc.

4720 Boston Way
Lanham, MD 20706

3 Henrietta Street
London WC2E 8LU England

Printed in the United States of America

ISBN (Perfect): 0-8191-3646-8

All University Press of America books are produced on acid-free
paper which exceeds the minimum standards set by the National
Historical Publications and Records Commission.

To Ann for her inspiration and
support and to Amy, Deb, Gary
and Scott for their expressions
of interest and pride in my work

Contents

1. Reading and Some Essentials of
    an Effective Reading Program 1

2. The Classroom Learning Environment 9

3. Relating Principles of Learning to
    Teaching of Reading 23

4. Word Recognition and Comprehension Skills
    Needed for Effective Reading 35

5. Various Approaches to Reading Instruction 51

6. Planning Reading Lessons 63

7. Classroom Management 73

8. Integrating Reading with the
    Total Language Arts Program 81

9. Diagnosis - Developing a Blueprint for Instruction 89

10. Correction-Using Diagnosis as a
    Blueprint for Instruction 103

    Appendices 115

    "Your Own Paper"
    (Answer Blanks for Pre-assessment and
      Evaluation Activities) 165
    References 209

    About the Author 213

Preface

This is a handbook on reading for classroom teachers. Since the focus is on practical ideas for classroom teaching of reading, the handbook is also appropriate for use in educational methods classes with prospective teachers. The book is not designed to give full treatment to any of the topics discussed. Instead, I have attempted to present some basic information that will be helpful to anyone who has embarked upon his/her personal inquiry into the field of reading. In this sense, it is a beginning for the reader interested in learning about the basics of reading instruction.

For the reader who is interested in a careful study of the material, pre-assessment and evaluation activities are provided. It is suggested that maximum benefit will be realized when the reader completes these activities in writing. The format is self-instructional with answer keys for the pre-assessment and evaluation activities provided in the appendices. In the back of the handbook, the reader will find blank sheets that can be torn out and used to complete the pre-assessment and evaluation activities.

The first thing the reader should do after reading this preface is to obtain a ruler to place along the dotted line on page 167 and tear out the answer blank on that page and also page 169. Before reading each chapter, the same procedure should be followed, i.e., pre-assessment and evaluation answer blanks should be torn out of the back of the book before the reading of each of the ten chapters.

If your reading of the handbook has a positive impact on your work with children and reading, then my purpose in writing the handbook will have been fulfilled.

R.C.P.

1

"Whatever the teacher believes about the nature of reading may have more impact than any other single factor upon the way in which the teacher helps children learn to read."

Reading and

Some Essentials

of an Effective

Classroom Reading

Program

CHAPTER ONE: Reading and Some Essentials of an Effective
                     Classroom Reading Program

I.   Directions for the study of the chapter:

     A.   Read the list of competencies to be developed in the
          chapter.

     B.   Complete the pre-assessment activities to help you set
          purposes for your reading.

     C.   Check your pre-assessment work with the appropriate
          key in the appendices.

     D.   Complete the reading activity.

     E.   Complete the evaluation for the chapter and check your
          work with the appropriate key in the appendices.

II. Competencies to be developed:

     Upon completion of this chapter, the reader will be able
     to:

     A.   Write a definition of reading.

     B.   Identify specific skills to be developed through
          classroom reading instruction.

     C.   Cite factors which affect reading growth.

     D.   Characterize the instructional, independent, and
          recreational aspects of a classroom reading program.

III. Pre-Assessment: Complete your pre-assessment on "YOUR OWN
     PAPER" page 167. When you finish, check your work with the
     KEY found in Appendix A Page 117.

     A.   Write a brief statement that answers the question
          "What is reading".

     B.   Identify at least three specific skills which need to
          be developed with children in a classroom reading
          program.

     C.   Identify 4 factors which affect reading growth.

     D.   What is the difference between the instructional and
          the independent aspects of a classroom reading
          program?

2

IV. Reading Activity:

One of the most important things a classroom teacher should do in preparation for classroom reading instruction is to accept or develop a meaningful definition of reading. Whatever the teacher believes about the nature of reading may have more impact than any other single factor upon the way in which the teacher helps children learn to read. Some teachers teach reading the way they do because they accept a definition which considers reading as a "set of skills." Others teach reading a certain way because they consider reading as a "meaning-making process" or because they consider reading to be a process of "perceiving, interpreting, and evaluating" printed material.

For our purposes here, reading can be defined as a process. It is a process of communication in which one person's ideas are exchanged with another person through the use of printed symbols. Further, it is a process involving physical abilities, decoding abilities, and thinking abilities. The teacher who accepts this kind of definition of reading will likely provide a reading program that focuses on the communication of ideas. As well, this teacher will simultaneously provide for the following as daily reading experiences are provided in the classroom:

1. Physical aspect - Reading is a physical process. It takes a great deal of energy to read, and the child needs good eyesight and eye movements as well as good auditory acuity and discrimination. The hungry or tired child can be expected to experience problems in reading. The child with visual and auditory problems will need those problems corrected before normal reading development can be expected. The classroom teacher who is concerned about the physical aspects of reading also sees to it that lighting, room arrangement, and the total classroom environment are appropriate as the daily classroom reading program is developed.

2. Decoding aspect - This aspect of the reading process is very important. The teacher who believes in its importance provides opportunities for children to read for meaning. Children also are provided with opportunities to discuss and analyze what they read. The teacher who believes in the importance of this aspect of reading will be the teacher who provides much time for independent and recreational reading activities throughout the school day thereby extending the reading period beyond the "reading circle."

3

The preceding definition is one of many which might be accepted by the classroom teacher. A perusal of major texts in the reading field will yield a variety of definitions to choose from. Regardless of the specific definition accepted, however, the teacher will find that concern needs to be directed at specific skill development at some point in the classroom reading program. Again, a variety of skill lists are available. Chapter four of this handbook will provide the classroom teacher with a brief discussion of the following selected major reading skills:

1. sight vocabulary development
2. context clues
3. phonetic analysis
4. structural analysis
5. reading to find main ideas
6. reading to select significant details
7. reading to follow directions
8. reading to answer questions
9. reading to summarize and organize
10. reading to arrive at generalizations
11. reading to evaluate critically
12. Reading to get meaning from phrases, sentences, and longer selections

In addition to accepting or developing a personal definition of reading and an awareness and understanding of specific skills required, the teacher also needs to maintain a serious concern and understanding of the various factors which affect or have an impact on normal reading growth. The classroom teacher needs to be willing to give consideration to the importance of such factors as the following ones cited by Bond, Tinker, and Wasson (1979) as causes of reading disability:

1. visual deficiency
2. auditory deficiency
3. speech defects
4. general health
5. intellectual limitations
6. personal and social adjustment
7. home environment
8. attitudes
9. cultural and language differences
10. lack of readiness for beginning reading instruction
11. methods of teaching

4

Other factors often cited as having a significant impact on reading growth are the sex of the child (Girls can be expected to do better than boys.), and experiential background. The point to be made here is that reading is a complex process having a variety of factors which impact or affect normal development of the process. Many of the factors cannot be identified through a reading test that might be administered. In order to understand a child's reading progress, the teacher may need information from sources outside of the classroom such as the home, medical doctor, psychologist, nurse or other teachers.

Once the classroom teacher "comes to grips" with a meaningful definition of reading, the skills involved, and some factors which affect reading, attention might well be directed at the essentials that need consideration in an effective reading program. Of greatest importance here is a recognition that there should be three major parts in an effective classroom reading program. Children should experience instructional activities, independent activities, and recreational reading activities.

The instructional part of the program is that part of the reading program through which the teacher provides children with the basic reading skills, attitudes, and appreciations in reading. In some cases, an instructional grade level can be found by administering a standardized reading test. The teacher, however, can most readily determine an instructional level by administering an Informal Reading Inventory. The criteria for establishing the instructional level is a 75% score on comprehension. In addition the child should be able to pronounce 95 out of 100 words, have natural, rhythmical, well phrased oral reading, and no observable tensions.

Following the determination of an instructional level, the teacher can then refer to the Barbe Reading Checklist in order to see the specific basic skills that should be developed at the particular grade level at which the child will receive instruction. Much of the instructional part of the reading program can be handled through grouping children for small group instruction. This is the part of the program most often treated with a basal reader which systematically provides for the continuity of basic skill development.

The independent part of the reading program is the part of the program in which the child is encouraged to read without direct teacher assistance to answer questions or complete a particular task. The classroom teacher can often provide these planned independent reading activities by planning such experiences in social studies, science, or some other curriculum area during the day. Multi-level materials such as the SRA Reading Lab, the EDL Study Skills Library, and Reader's Digest materials can also be utilized to provide children with supervised independent reading. This is the part of the program where the children can practice the skills they learn in the instructional part of the program. It is the part of the program where the children begin to see the practical need for well developed skills in the reading process. The Informal Reading Inventory can be used to determine the independent level. The criteria for making this determination is a 90% score on comprehension. In addition the child should be able to pronounce 99 out of 100 running words, have natural, rhythmical, well phrased oral reading, and no observable tensions.

The recreational reading part of the program is that part of the program in which the teacher encourages children to really enjoy reading, to explore present interests through reading, to delve into new interests, and to generally develop the habit of reading as a pleasurable activity. This is the part of the reading program in which the classroom teacher needs to work with the librarian to help children find access to the reading material that will match the varied needs of children. The teacher can enhance this part of the program by building classroom book collections, reading to children, and reading his/her favorite book in front of children while they read their books. One of the best ways to help children enjoy their recreational reading is to provide 30-60 minutes for recreational reading immediately following each visit to the library. The chances of a child enjoying and finishing a library book may well be best immediately following the selection of the book. No particular test will need to be administered in order to determine the recreational reading level. For most cases the teacher can guide children to books at or below the independent reading level. However, another consideration is the interest the children have for various topics. The focus should be on providing time for children to read what they enjoy so that upon leaving the school environment, they will choose to read and gain much lifetime pleasure from their involvement with the process of reading.

V. Evaluation:

   A. On "YOUR OWN PAPER" Page 169, answer the following questions. When you finish, check your work with the KEY found in Appendix B page 121. Assign 10 points to each question you answer correctly.

1-3. According to the definition of reading offered in the chapter, what three types of general abilities are needed for success in the reading process?

4-6. List 3 specific skills which need to be developed with children in a classroom reading program.

7-9. Identify 2 factors which have been determined to affect reading growth with children.

10. Through the use of an Informal Reading Inventory, the teacher can determine the instructional and independent reading levels of children. Which level is the level at which the child achieves a 90% score on comprehension and is able to pronounce 99 out of 100 running words?

B. If you do not achieve a score of at least 90%, you may want to re-read portions of the chapter.

2

"Children should be learning, and most
specifically, learning to read in an
environment which is consistent with the
society in which we are teaching them to
live."

The Classroom

Learning

Environment

CHAPTER TWO: The Classroom Learning Environment

I.   Directions for the study of the chapter:

    A.   Read the list of competencies to be developed in the chapter.

    B.   Complete the pre-assessment activities to help you set purposes for your reading.

    C.   Check your pre-assessment work with the appropriate key in the appendices.

    D.   Complete the reading activity.

    E.   Complete the evaluation for the chapter and check your work with the appropriate key in the appendices.

II.   Competencies to be developed:

Upon completion of this chapter, the reader will be able to:

    A.   Identify 5 typical characteristics of an informal and democratic "open" learning environment.

    B.   Identify 5 typical freedoms and corresponding responsibilities that might be given to children in a democratic classroom learning environment.

III.   Pre-assessment: Complete your pre-assessment on "YOUR OWN PAPER" Page 171. When you finish, check your work with the KEY found in Appendix C page 123.

    A.   List 5 typical characteristics of an informal and democratic "open" learning environment.

    B.   List 5 typical freedoms and corresponding responsibilities that might be given to children in a democratic classroom learning environment.

IV. Reading Activity:

According to Hurt, Scott, and McCroskey (1978), there are no cookbook strategies that teachers can turn to in their attempt to help children in satisfying all of their intellectual and academic needs. According to them, the research does suggest, however, that children seem to be better adjusted and to develop more favorable attitudes toward the total learning environment when the teacher's leadership style is democratic. It is the position of this writer that reading development can be enhanced when the teacher develops some form of a democratic classroom environment. One form of a democratic environment has been offered by Guenther (1972) and was referred to as an "open" learning environment. According to Guenther, such a learning environment involves:

1. Open-minded, open ended learning opportunities for all children to learn to the maximum of their capacities to learn, in accordance with their individual levels of development, their interests, problems, and need for learning.

2. Carefully planned, purposefully organized, broadly evaluated, genuine child-centered education --- with or without open spaces.

3. Showing authentic respect for each individual and his or her ideas.

4. Having sincere faith in every child's ability and desire to learn.

5. Believing that children can learn ordered freedom and can develop responsibility for their own conduct and learning.

6. Confidence that satisfaction in achievement and true pleasure in learning result when the learner sees real purpose for, and personal meaning in, the learning.

7. A spider-web approach which fosters multi-dimensional opportunities for learning.

In general the approach suggested by Guenther involves an open-minded attitude toward learning and all learners.

As other writers have discussed such a democratic classroom environment, they seem to adhere to the following criteria:

1. Freedom of movement for children

2. Use of learning centers

3. Pupil teacher planning

4. Individualization of instruction through learning options provided in the classroom environment.
5. Flexibility in scheduling of daily learning activities.

It seems to this writer, that in our modern schools of today, children should be learning, and most specifically, learning to read in an environment which is consistent with the society in which we are teaching children to live. Perhaps, in some classroom situations, we are teaching pupils in environments which resemble a dictatorship rather than a democracy. That is to say, that is some instances, the environment is one in which the teacher makes all decisions, evaluates all behavior, takes the consequences for all successes and failures, and even takes the sole responsibility for a well organized and immaculate classroom. We cannot, it seems to me, help children learn to become responsible freedom-loving persons if we do not give them freedoms and responsibilities in a democratic classroom atmosphere.

Keep in mind that there are no cookbook strategies that you can turn to in establishing the "proper" learning environment. However, you may find encouragement and practical ideas in establishing such a democratic environment through my sharing with you the following strategy this writer has used to establish such an environment with a fifth grade class.

Our classroom democracy was initiated early in the school year, following a discussion of what democracy really means. It was fairly well agreed that it was a manner of living together in which we have many freedoms but also corresponding responsibilities. One sample listed on the chalkboard was the right to vote. The corresponding responsibility was, then, that we should vote in a democracy. Charts were also constructed by individual pupils on which they listed freedoms and responsibilities that they felt were evident in their individual homes. Later, the classroom organization was discussed, and a chart was constructed which listed freedoms that the pupils felt they wanted, as well as the corresponding responsibilities they should have if the classroom was really going to resemble their outside world. One freedom that was listed was the freedom to do individual research. The corresponding responsibility was to then share the findings with other members of the class. This chart was posted in the back of the classroom and referred to regularly as we found the need to discuss the room-management or clarify our roles as members of the classroom democracy. The chart which was posted and served as a guide included these other following freedoms and responsibilities:

Freedoms	Responsibilities
To read freely	...... To record and share
To get drinks and use the lavatory	...... To be quiet when doing so
To get materials and work independently	...... To work quietly so others can work
To ask questions and to ask for help	...... To think before asking
To hold group discussions	...... To talk softly
To express our ideas	...... To listen while others express their ideas
To sit and work in groups	...... To cooperate with group leaders

During the first month of school, reading groups were established based upon standardized and informal test results. The classroom was then arranged so that it took on the appearance of four reading "tables." Since in our American Democracy the president appoints those he feels can best handle a job, the teacher appointed four group leaders. We were now on our way to a form of classroom organization that at least could resemble a kind of representative government. This grouping process became an important element in our democratic classroom. Pupils appeared to learn much about working together with guidance from the group leaders and teacher. The group leaders were changed each week so that everyone got a chance to practice leadership. Some of the responsibilities of the group leaders included:

Taking of group attendance
Taking of group lunch count
Distribution and collection of materials

13

Leading of group discussions
Supervision of group during study periods
Discussion of group problems with teacher

In addition, it was agreed that each pupil should have some specific responsibility for helping to manage the classroom. Board washers, window adjusters, file clerks, librarians, and others were appointed. Each pupil took care of his/her classroom responsibility at the end of each day. At the end of each week the pupils helped clean the classroom from "stem to stern." Pupils took pride in these jobs, and had an opportunity to exercise their responsibilities with authority.

The pupils were taught the basic program and had an enrichment and supplementary program that they might have had in any typical classroom. However, the rewarding difference was that they became a part of the governing of the classroom and took much pride in all that was accomplished. The pupils did not "run" the classroom nor its educational program. When problems could not be solved by the pupils working together, and any other time authority was needed, the teacher was quick to administer it. The implementation of a classroom democracy did not mean that no authority was exercised by the teacher. Just as in our American Democracy, authority was exercised when it was needed to protect the rights and property of others.

It has been demonstrated to me, through classroom experiences such as previously discussed, that children and teachers can live and learn in a classroom in accordance with pupil-teacher established freedoms and responsibilities. My own classroom experience has revealed to me that there are general things that can be done to enhance the total democratic learning environment and also specific things that can be done to enhance the environment for classroom reading.

General Recommendations

Since various reading-learning activities occur throughout the school day, the teacher needs to be concerned with the total learning environment and should consider the establishment of some form of democratic environment as classroom management is planned. The following are some recommendations the classroom teacher might consider:

1.   Seat children in groups throughout the day.

        When children area seated in groups, they learn
        to live with others in a way consistent with the
        outside world. This arrangement provides opportun-

ities for the use of language to solve problems and relate to others in a natural way. Group leaders can help keep the groups to the tasks at hand. Group leaders can also assist the teacher by leading group discussions, collecting and distributing papers, taking lunch count, and helping members of the groups as they have questions related to daily routines.

2. Move the teacher's desk away from the front of the room.

Having the teacher's desk in the front of the room can help develop a feeling of control. However, it can also impede the development of appreciation for democratic living. When the teacher's desk is placed in the back or on the side of the classroom, the children can begin to rely more upon each other as they live and learn together. This arrangement can do a great deal toward helping the children feel that the classroom is a place for them to learn together.

3. Provide for open discussion at the beginning of each day.

Children will have personal matters to share and discuss each day. If the teacher does not provide time for such oral expression at the beginning of each day, the children will still engage in such oral expression. The problem arises when such oral expression occurs during structured lessons throughout the day. In fifteen minutes each morning, the teacher and children can share in oral expression then "get down" to the various other learning tasks to be completed.

4. Assign classroom jobs to each child.

There are many routine tasks that must receive attention each day within the classroom. Children can learn to share these tasks and take additional pride in the classroom when they are permitted to take part in the completion of routine tasks. This can also "free" the teacher to give individualized instruction as needed. In some cases, teachers have found it useful to discuss and assign routine tasks and then post them on a chart in the room.

5. Provide an atmosphere of sharing by reading to the children.

   Since children tend to do what they see adults do, it is often a good idea for the children to see the teacher engaged in reading activities. Seeing the teacher enjoy such activities, can also help develop a favorable attitude toward learning and the habit of reading.

6. Have classroom meetings to discuss and resolve classroom problems as they arise.

   Throughout the typical classroom day, problems arise and decisions must be made to resolve these problems. Too often, children see the teacher making these decisions. Whenever possible, children should be given opportunities to engage in the resolutions of such problems. This can help them develop positive feelings toward themselves and their place in a democratic scheme.

7. Post a chart of classroom freedoms and responsibilities.

   Most children will learn to cherish the informality and openness of the democratic classroom environment. However, they often need to be reminded of their specific roles in such an environment. A chart of freedoms and responsibilities can help remind them of their freedoms but also serves as a reminder of the responsibilities that correspond with each of the freedoms they enjoy.

8. Arrange materials and equipment for effective use by the children.

   Putting children in close proximity to the materials and equipment they most often need for learning can help "cut down" on noise, confusion, and distractions in a classroom. Without this provision, the democratic environment can become unmanageable. As well as grouping children, the teacher might well plan to group materials and equipment so they are at maximum accessibility to the children who need them. This can also include an effort to make materials and extra classroom supplies available to children in a central location.

9. Allow children to assist with record keeping.

        The development of a democratic environment can
    often result in more individualized learning
    activities. Such activities can often result in more
    papers to correct and more record keeping chores for
    the teacher. The teacher can obtain some relief in
    this area by having children correct some of their own
    practice papers. This can be accomplished by taping 2
    or 3 keys to written exercises on selected desks
    around the room. When children finish their written
    exercises, they can correct their practice work and
    get immediate reinforcement to enhance learning.
    Children can also keep folders of work and progress
    charts to help you and them "keep track" of progress.

10. Organize an independent research lab period

        A learning environment in which children can
    explore some of their own interests can be a learning
    environment in which all learning is enhanced. Con-
    sideration might well be given to one 30-45 minute
    period each week during which children can work on an
    area of interest. This period can lead children into
    an integration of learnings as they pursue art
    projects, research topics, or construction activities.

Specific Recommendations for Reading

    Learning to read in a democratic classroom environment can
lead to increased skills development, expanded reading interests, and improvement in the reading habit. The following are
some recommendations the classroom teacher might consider as
total reading abilities are enhanced in a democratic learning
environment:

1. Establish a recreational reading center.

        Classroom book collections have long been made avail-
    able by classroom teachers. This is a good practice and
    gives recreational reading a priority place in the class-
    room. Such an area in the classroom can be stocked with
    library books that fit the interests of children in the
    room, favorite paper backs contributed by children, and
    other materials that fit children's interests such as
    travel brochures, cookbooks, magazines, and free and
    inexpensive materials available in the community.

2. Allow children to write stories that can be signed out and read by other children.

   When children write a story, they often take great pride in it and want to share it with others. The teacher can help the child place the story in a manila folder and place a circulation card in the back. The child can also make an attractive cover and place the story on a rack or table in the recreational reading center for other children to read. At times, a classroom collection of such stories can even be placed in a designated area in the school library for circulation to other children in the school. This activity can help children develop a sense of reading as a process of communicating ideas to others. In general, it may help the children develop an appreciation for the written word that can "carry over" to all reading activities.

3. Allow children to read to each other.

   Rather than emphasizing "round robin" oral reading during instruction time, the teacher might consider having children read to each other in pairs and small groups as they practice oral reading. This can be much less threatening to children and can put oral reading into a relaxed and enjoyable context. At times, this practice can also help provide incentive to good readers as they read to those who find reading to be a difficult process.

4. Develop individualized folders for use by children in free time.

   The effective classroom teacher is well aware of the merits of keeping children constructively involved. The problem often arises when the teacher begins to search for materials to serve this purpose. Teacher made materials can often be superior aids to use with children when they finish assigned work. There are several activity books currently on the market that can provide appropriate activities. One way the teacher can get children interested in such activities is to redesign activities to fit into a standard manila folder. A colorful picture can be placed on the folder to motivate the child. Written directions can be placed on the inside of the cover. With young children, directions can be placed on a cassette tape and put on the inside of the cover page. The activity can be fitted to the other page on the inside of the folder, and a correction key can be placed on the back of the folder. Such self-instructional and self correction activities can be keyed to the needs of a particular class and help the teacher provide practice activities in reading skills.

5. **Provide time for recreational reading immediately following the library period.**

    Perhaps, the best time to interest children in recreational reading is immediately following their personal selection of a book. Following the library period, the teacher might consider a 30-45 minute classroom period during which all children begin the reading of the books they have selected. The teacher might also serve as a good role model by reading his or her own book during this time.

6. **Provide relaxation areas for recreational reading.**

    In addition to the establishment of a recreational reading center, the teacher might consider the designation of a few selected areas as areas for recreational reading. A few bean bag chairs, a rocking chair, or an old lawn chair or two can help children to relax and escape into the world of reading. These areas can be made available to children throughout the day.

7. **Utilize brochures and other free advertising materials at interest level of children.**

    Some children often reject the typical school reading materials. Such children can sometimes be motivated to engage in the reading process through brochures from local farm supply stores, automobile dealers, and other commercial sources in the community.

8. **Make a "When all is said and done" bulletin board.**

    When children finish their assigned tasks, they sometimes do not know what activities they can engage in to make good use of their time. The teacher can make a bulletin board with the caption "When all is said and done." The teacher can place on the bulletin board various enrichment reading activities to provide children with experiences in independent reading.

9. Provide independent and recreational reading activities for groups while instructional activities are being provided for another group.

    More than one basal reading lesson has ended in ruins because of the teacher's lack of ability to conduct 3 or more instructional lessons during the same period. One way to avoid this might be to have one group receive direct instruction while other groups are engaged in independent and recreational activities. The teacher may not complete as many instructional periods per week, but the quality of such lessons is sure to be enhanced.

10. Make use of a daily log sheet.

    Children do seem to enjoy talking about the activities they engage in during the school day. The teacher can capitalize on this by running enough copies of a ditto "Daily Log Sheet" to be used each day of the school year. Each sheet can contain blanks or spaces for the following:

    a. today's weather
    b. children absent today
    c. today's assignments
    d. the most important things we learned today

    Each day a child can be selected to take notes during the day and to complete the "Daily Log Sheet." At the end of the day, the child can read the report to the class and any corrections or additions can be made. In addition, the sheets can be placed in a large log book in the room each day. When children return from being absent they can read the sheets for the days missed and thereby obtain all assignments. The large daily log can also be shared with any classroom visitors to show what the class has been doing.

V. Evaluation:

    A. On "YOUR OWN PAPER" page 173, answer the following questions. When you finish, check your work with the KEY found in Appendix D page 125. Assign 10 points to each question you answer correctly.

        1-5 List 5 typical characteristics of an informal and democratic "open" learning environment.

6-10 List 5 typical freedoms and corresponding responsibilities that might be given to children in a democratic classroom environment.

B. If you do not achieve a score of at least 90%, you may want to re-read portions of this chapter.

3

"Your success in teaching reading will be enhanced when you can implement the time tested principles of learning in the work you do with children in your classroom."

Relating Principles

of Learning to

Teaching of Reading

CHAPTER THREE: Relating Principles of Learning to Teaching of
                Reading

I.   Directions for study of the chapter:

     A.   Read the list of competencies to be developed in the
          chapter.

     B.   Complete the pre-assessment activities to help you set
          purposes for your reading.

     C.   Check your pre-assessment work with the appropriate
          key in the appendices.

     D.   Complete the reading activity.

     E.   Complete the evaluation for the chapter and check your
          work with the appropriate key in the appendices.

II. Competencies to be developed:

     Upon completion of this chapter, the reader will be able
     to:

     A.   Identify various motivational techniques that can be
          used in reading instruction.

     B.   Identify various means of helping children relate what
          they learn during reading instruction with the outside
          world.

     C.   Identify various ways to maximize pupil participation
          in reading lessons.

     D.   Identify various ways to get children to transfer what
          they learn in reading to other subject areas.

     E.   Identify various ways to evaluate pupil progress in
          the reading program.

III. Complete your pre-assessment on "YOUR OWN PAPER" page 175.
     When you finish, check your work with the KEY found in
     Appendix E page 127.

     A.   List as many principles of learning as you can.

     B.   Identify at least two different ways that teachers can
          motivate children to learn.

24

C. Identify two factors that you think you might consider if you were going to evaluate and grade children in the area of reading.

IV. Reading Activity:

One of the interesting observations one might make about teachers and their training is that they train for at least four years to learn how to teach. Many of them leave this training behind and teach the way they want to anyway, often with little regard for the application of principles and methods they learned through their training program. When this happens, it is unfortunate, since there are accepted principles which, over the years, have been demonstrated to work in improving the teaching-learning situation. Your success in teaching reading will be enhanced when you implement the "time tested" principles in the work you do with children in your classroom. Although there are many such principles of learning, and just as many ways of stating them, the intent here is to simply suggest a few of the more subtle principles and the manner in which you might implement them as you work with reading in your classroom.

Self-Need Motivation:

The principle of self-need motivation suggests that the chances of learning taking place are enhanced when the teacher "gets the children ready" for what he/she wants the class to learn. This principle further suggests that children will probably learn better when they are interested in what is being taught to them. It is, of course, the teacher's job to help the children get interested in what it is that they are to learn. To do this, the teacher can use a variety of motivational techniques. Some of these techniques include goal setting, building upon previous experience, the use of concrete objects, curiosity, and fear.

1. Goal setting can often be an effective means of motivating pupils. As you utilize this technique, you help set goals for the pupils so that they will be interested enough in the teaching that follows to pay close attention. This can be done by writing questions on the chalkboard and asking children to try to answer the questions before reading a selection. For example, if the children were reading a selection that had something to do with Egypt at the intermediate grade level, the teacher might put the following questions on the chalkboard:

    a. Why is Egypt called the "gift of the Nile?"
    b. What is a shadoof?
    c. Why did civilization develop along the Nile?

As the teacher introduces the lesson, pupils could be asked
to look at the questions and to try to answer them.
Chances are that they will not be able to supply complete
answers to the questions before reading the assigned material. It is at this point that the teacher then sets goals
for the children by saying "At the end of our reading
lesson today, we should be able to answer all of the
questions on the chalkboard." This very often will help to
get the attention of the children and motivate them for
what is to follow. Another example of goal setting as a
motivational technique that might be appropriate for use
with individual children and small groups is when the
teacher puts up a map of the United States and has children
start on the East Coast and move toward the West Coast by
placing a small paper car on the map each time a book is
read by the individual or member of a small group. The
goal is to place the paper cars end to end to form a
continuous chain from the East Coast to the West Coast
and to see which child can do it first.

    In the democratic classroom environment, where indivi-
dualization of instruction is prevalent, teachers often
have children keep progress charts in reading. Children
are encouraged to set realistic goals for themselves and to
monitor their progress as they complete, check, and grade
various reading exercises. Other times, the emphasis is on
setting goals for children and helping them set their own
goals. For many children, goal setting is a powerful
motivational technique that tends to motivate them to
learn.

2. Building upon previous experience is often a good way to
    motivate children. When the teacher begins a lesson with
    an individual child, a small group, or the total group with
    something with which the individual or group is familiar,
    learners often feel comfortable and ready to learn more
    about any given topic. To better understand this
    motivational technique, you might assume that you wanted to
    introduce children to a story titled Larry the Lion. In
    using previous experience as a motivational technique, you
    might begin the lesson by simply asking a series of
    questions such as:

a. How many of you have ever been to a zoo?
b. What was the funniest animal you saw at the zoo? (Let the children discuss.)
c. What was the strangest animal you saw at the zoo? (Let the children discuss.)
d. What was the bravest animal you saw at the zoo? (Let the children discuss.)

You might then inform the children that "today, we are going to read a story about one of the bravest animals of all. Let's open our reading books to page 6 to the story titled Larry the Lion and read to find what made Larry so brave." The time spend building upon the previous experience of children can often serve to get them interested in the lesson that you plan to develop with the children.

3. The use of concrete objects can often help you motivate children for their reading lesson. Concrete objects that in some way relate to your lesson can often be used. For example, if the children were going to read a story about "cowboys and the old west," you might bring in some object like a toy gun, a holster, a cowboy hat, or some other object that the children might associate with "cowboys and the old west." In order to get the children excited about the activity, you might put the object in a box or cover it over so pupils cannot see what it is. They might be asked to shake it, lift it, and even feel it as they try to guess what it is. Once they have identified the object, you can encourage them to discuss it in such a way that the discussion will lead them to become motivated about "cowboys and the old west." When this point has been reached, the class can be referred to the story for the day. The use of the object to touch off the discussion should help get the children motivated for the story which is to follow.

4. Curiosity can often become an effective means of motivating young children for reading instruction. For example, when introducing a phonics lesson on the vowel-consonant-final e pattern in a word, the teacher might place the following words on the blackboard:

coke

cake

rope

hike

28

The teacher can then ask "What things do these four words have in common with each other?" After the children use their curiosity in examining the words, the teacher can lead the children to the generalization regarding the vowel-consonant-final e pattern in words, and solicit other words from the children that they feel fit the pattern. Another way to use curiosity is to have children discuss each of the pictures in a story as they try to tell what they think might be happening in a story. They can then read the story and see whether or not their predictions were correct.

5. Although _fear_ is not the best technique to use for motivating children, there are times when its use might be justifiable. When this motivational technique is used, the teacher suggests that pupils will not be able to participate in some pleasurable activity unless they "pay attention and succeed," in some specific learning situation. An example of this technique would be when a teacher introduces a follow-up activity, such as answering ten specific detail questions, which must be done carefully and completely and a certain score achieved before being permitted to engage in the free reading period which is to follow. As the assignment is made, the teacher might indicate that all pupils who fail to answer questions correctly will have to spend time writing and doing further study while the remainder of the class has a free reading period. The planned motivation might well end with "Now let's work carefully and do a good job on the questions so we can all enjoy our free reading period."

The Principle of Association:

The principle of association suggests that learning is enhanced when the teacher sprinkles learning activities with illustrations within the outside world experiences of the children. The following list of examples has been developed to give you some ideas on how you might use the principle of association as you teach reading in your classroom:

1. Have children think of people they know who reflect some of the qualities of characters they read about in stories used for reading instruction.

2. Incorporate into your follow-up assignments opportunities to observe and draw upon experiences in the home and the community.

3. Try to draw upon and refer to things children have seen or will see on television in their own homes.

28836

4.   As you work with word recognition skills, have children make a booklet of words relating to a personal interest or hobby. For example, a child with an interest in transportation could build a transportation alphabet. Each page of a booklet could contain a letter of the alphabet, a picture related to the word, the word naming the picture, and a sentence using the word. The word can also be analyzed by marking vowel sounds and syllabication. Such an activity can help the child see how what he/she is learning in classroom reading instruction is related to his/her real world of interests outside of the classroom.

5.   Local newspapers and classroom current events weekly papers can be utilized to show children how their increasing ability to read can help them understand the real world around them.

6.   Have children bring in a menu from a restaurant, cereal boxes, tour pamphlets, and other reading material they encounter in their real world. Place such materials in a learning center in the room with exercises that will help them develop the word recognition and comprehension skills being developed in the classroom reading program.

The Principle of Self-Activity:

The principle of self-activity suggests that the chances of learning taking place are enhanced when the learners are encouraged to take an active part in the lessons being taught. This implies that pupils be encouraged to discuss, answer question, and present their views in the reading lessons that you teach. The classroom teacher needs to have a variety of activities at his/her disposal that can be utilized as an attempt is made to maximize pupil participation in reading lessons. The following suggestions should be helpful:

1.   Plan to have children do a number of plays as a part of the reading instructional program. Plays magazine is a good source of short plays appropriate for use in the elementary school classroom. Rather than having a few major "productions" each school year, have the children participate in reading by reading and acting out several plays within the classroom. Word recognition and comprehension skills can easily be reinforced through this reading activity.

2.   After the reading of a story, have children form pairs and interview each other in regard to the plot and characters in the story.

30

3. Have children who are good readers read stories on tape to be shared with lower grade children. Lower grade teachers are often very cooperative in such an endeavor.

4. Ask children to write down words they find difficult in a story and have them discuss the words with the class after the story is read.

5. Indentify children who have mastered specific word recognition and comprehension skills and have them serve as "peer teachers" to children needing help with specific skills. A period each day or each week can be set aside for such participation as children help teach each other reading skills.

6. Develop a weekly or monthly classroom newsletter in which children can use their language and reading skills to compile relevant reading material for each other.

7. Utilize multi-level kits of materials which enable children to participate in the selection, administration, and scoring of reading exercises.

8. During a reading lesson, ask children to "act out" the story.

9. Allow children to assist in the building of classroom reading collections and the development of reading learning centers and bulletin boards.

10. Allow children to record material regarding class discussions on the chalkboard instead of you always using the chalkboard for such activity. Let them put your notes, new words, etc. on the board prior to a lesson you plan to teach.

The Principle of Transfer:

This principle of learning suggests that learning will be enhanced when we get children to transfer their learning from one subject area to another within the total instructional program. This has a particular implications for the reading teacher in the classroom where opportunities exist to have children apply their reading abilities to all other subject areas during the day.

One very effective way to help children transfer what they learn in reading to other subject areas is to teach children to utilize a work study skill technique as they read materials in science, math, and social studies. While several such

31

techniques are available, the following technique is suggested for your use in an intermediate level classroom. Children can be taught to follow the following steps when reading all material in all subject areas:

1. Appraise background of experience - The children ask themselves what they might already know about a particular subject and begin to organize their experiential background that they can bring to bear upon their reading assignment.

2. Preview - Children are taught to quickly go through any reading material looking at maps, graphs, charts, and other aids. They also can be taught to skim the first sentence of each paragraph.

3. Question - This usually takes place at the time the children are previewing. They begin to raise questions about the material so they will be looking for something while reading.

4. Read - Children now read the material silently as they bring their background to bear upon the material, bring their general knowledge about the topic to bear upon the material, and look for answers to their own questions.

5. Review - Children are taught to go back over the material to see if they can recall what they had read.

6. Check Comprehension - The children are now ready to complete a comprehension exercise in the book or one devised by the teacher. The intent is that the steps followed in the work study skill technique will help them better understand the material read.

When children in an intermediate grade level classroom are taught such a technique, they can often better utilize their existing reading abilities and transfer their learning of reading skills to all subject areas.

The EDL Study Skills Library materials, available from Educational Developmental Laboratories, utilize the technique and are very useful in the classroom.

At the lower grade level, the teacher needs to use every opportunity to have children practice skills learned in the reading program as they work in all other subjects throughout the school day.

The Principle of Effect:

The principle of effect indicates that chances are good that learning will be enhanced when the teacher praises pupil responses. The following suggestions should be helpful to you as you attempt to praise the responses of children during reading instruction:

1. When you ask a child to answer a question, and he/she gives you a weak answer, you might say "Well that is a good try John. Listen for a moment and find out if we can get someone to expand that just a little further."

2. When a child reads orally during a lesson and misses a few words, don't point out that he/she missed three words. Instead . . . say "Very good John." You were able to get almost all of the words correct in your reading today."

3. When children do a good job on a written assignment, write a pleasant comment on the work indicating that the child did a good job. Such comments might include . . . "You can be proud of your work on this paper." You might also write . . . "You did a very nice job and should feel good about this paper."

4. During oral reading sessions, thank children and make positive comments about their reading.

5. Give children opportunities to read a book to the class in installments. Praise them for their efforts.

The Principle of Evaluation:

This principle of learning indicates that learning activities and progress should be evaluated in a way that is consistent with the objectives the teacher had in mind for emphasis in a particular lesson. Before any lesson is taught to children, the teacher should specify objectives on paper or in his/her head. For example, the teacher may specify that: At the conclusion of the lesson, children will be able to:

1. Identify, in writing, four main events that occurred in the story titled The Railroad Cat.

2. Use the term conveyor belt in a sentence in a way that shows the proper meaning of the term.

In order to evaluate whether or not the children experienced a successful lesson, the teacher should evaluate by asking the children to do the two things stated in the above objectives. At all times, the teacher needs to go back to stated objectives as a basis for the evaluation that is to be done.

V.   Evaluation:

    A.   On "YOUR OWN PAPER" page 177, answer the following
         questions. When you finish, check your work with the
         KEY found in Appendix F page 131. Assign 10 points to
         each question you answer correctly.

        1-5 . . . List five principles of learning.

        6   . . . When a teacher introduces a lesson with an
                 imaginative object in a box, he/she is using
                 the principle of _____.
        7-9 . . . List three techniques that can be used to
                 motivate children's learning.
        10 . . . When a teacher praises pupil responses,
                 he/she   is   using   the   principle   of

                 _____.

    B.   If you do not achieve a score of at least 90%, you may
         want to re-read portions of this chapter.

4

"Reading involves much more than word recognition, however the ability to recognize written words is basic to the reading process."

Word Recognition and

Comprehension Skills

Needed for

Effective Reading

CHAPTER FOUR: Word Recognition and Comprehension Skills Needed
for Effective Reading

I.   Directions for the study of the chapter:

    A.   Read the list of competencies to be developed in the chapter.

    B.   Complete the pre-assessment activities to help set purposes for your reading.

    C.   Check your pre-assessment work with the appropriate key in the appendices.

    D.   Complete the reading activity.

    E.   Complete the evaluation for the chapter and check your work with the appropriate key in the appendices.

II. Competencies to be developed:

Upon completion of this chapter, the reader will be able to:

    A.   Identify word recognition skills needed by elementary school children for effective reading.

    B.   Identify comprehension skills needed by elementary school children for effective reading.

III. Pre-Assessment: Complete your pre-assessment on "YOUR OWN PAPER" page 179. When you finish, check your work with the KEY found in Appendix G page 133.

    A.   One of the skills a child needs in order to read is the ability to unlock unfamiliar words. List three word recognition skills or techniques that can be used to unlock unfamiliar words in reading.

    B.   The effective reader is able to get meaning from the printed word and to therefore comprehend what has been read. List four specific comprehension skills that are needed by the effective reader.

    C.   Which of the following is not a consonant blend?

        (a) bl   (b) ph   (c) fl   (d) sn

D. Which of the following words contains a diphthong?

    (a) house   (b) beat   (c) ride   (d) soap

E. Which of the following words contains an open syllable?

    (a) gobble   (b) sit   (c) table   (d) picture

IV. Reading Activity:

Word Recognition Skills:

Reading involves much more than word recognition, however, the ability to recognize written words is basic to the reading process. Without skill in associating word forms as given in writing with word sounds and meanings, the child cannot become an effective reader. Persons in the field of reading seem to accept, without much question, that this ability to recognize words is essential to the development of maturity in reading. There does not seem to be much argument with this point. However, there are many points of controversy concerning how word recognition should best be taught.

According to Dallmann, Rouch, Chang and DeBoer (1974):

> . . . The current debate among those in the reading field primarily focuses on the question of how word recognition should be taught in beginning reading instruction. The issue concerns whether the emphasis in the initial stages of reading instruction should be on learning the sounds represented by the written letters or whether, without much or any attention to the letter-sound relation, the effort should be concentrated on helping pupils to acquire the meaning of the written message. In other words, the point of contention is whether a code approach or a meaning approach to reading instruction should be used (p. 107).

Many people would state that the issue in beginning reading instruction is the "phonic system" versus the "look-say" approach. The intent here is to turn attention to the following major skills for developing independence in word recognition regardless of what approach is taken to reading instruction. The classroom teacher will probably find himself/herself using a variety and mixture of approaches and will need to be able to define and work with the following:

1. The development of sight vocabulary

2. The use of context clues

3. The use of phonetic and structural analysis

While the dictionary is not discussed here, it also is an aid to children as they attempt to unlock unfamiliar words.

Sight Vocabulary:

The value of the use of sight vocabulary, or what is sometimes called the whole-word method, was established by research studies that indicated in a single fixation, or involuntary stoppage of the eye, the reader recognizes whole words and even phrases that have become familiar to him/her through frequent exposure to them. Many reading systems begin with whole words and introduce the child to them through telling the words, associating the words with pictures, and using experience charts. As this word recognition technique is developed, words are often put on flashcards and flashed to children until they, in effect, memorize the words instantly without any analysis. Actually, in all reading instructional programs, the teacher works to develop an ever increasing sight vocabulary that can be called upon during reading. In beginning reading instruction, the Dolch 220 Word List is often put on flash cards and used with children. The development of this store of 220 words often precedes formal reading instruction in the primary grades. While sight vocabulary development is most important in initial reading instruction, it is also important to note that we are all constantly adding words to our sight vocabulary. A large meaningful sight vocabulary is a real aid to the effective reader at all levels.

Context clues

It is no accident that publishers put so many colorful pictures in books to be read by children. Children can be taught to use these pictures to help them recognize words that may be difficult for them. You should plan to have children use pictures in this way as you attempt to help them build a store of techniques that can be used to recognize words in their reading.

A word can also be recognized through the use of verbal context clues. For example, if the pupils know all of the words except ball in:

Hit the ball with the bat.

The teacher might tell them that he/she thinks many of them can figure where the new word appears. If the pupils suggest that the word might be ball, he/she will need to tell them that they are right. If the pupils do not name the correct word, the teacher should tell them the word, and help them see that ball fits with the meaning of the rest of the sentence.

Phonetic and Structural Analysis

Phonetics is the science that deals with the study of the sound system of any language. There is actually an international phonetic alphabet that is used in such study. Phonics is the application of phonetic knowledge to the teaching of reading and spelling. It is important for you to be able to work with phonics in the classroom. You also need to remember that phonics involves both phonetic and structural analysis of words. Phonetic analysis involves the analysis of individual sounds or phonemes in words, while structural analysis involves work with parts of words and includes prefixes, suffixes, root words, and syllabication. Unlike other word recognition techniques, phonics does require a specific body of knowledge on the part of the classroom teacher. The following information regarding phonetic and structural analysis is intended for the teacher's background before working with the children and materials that may be found in the classroom. While the material will not always be taught directly to children, the teacher needs to have an adequate background of the material.

PHONETIC AND STRUCTURAL ANALYSIS*

CONSANANTS

1. **Blends** - two or three consonants blended so closely that they are produced as one sound.

bl	dr	tw	squ	sm	sn	st	sc	sk	sp
gl	pr	sw							
fl	br								
cl	gr								
pl	tr								
sl	fr		Examples:	black		twin
spl	shr			splash		swarm
	thr			free		squash
	spr			shrink		snail
	str			string		skit
	scr					

2. **Digraphs** - two consonant letters that represent a single speech sound.

sh   th   wh   na   ph   gh   kn   ch
Examples: church   shirt   wheel   rang   rough   graph

3. **Silent Consonants** - Some consonants are silent when in combination with other letters.

mb   bt   gh   kh   ps   rh
Examples: lamb   debt   khaki   rhubarb
          hymn   psalm   witch

4. The th digraph has two common sounds (the voiced and unvoiced)

Voiced Examples: this   their   they   though   that
Unvoiced Examples: thing   thank   thimble   thick   third

VOWELS

Rules for Single Vowels

1. When the only vowel in a word or accented syllable is any place but the end of the word, it has a short sound.

    Examples: ran   bet   shot   hut

*Included with permission of Dr. Gerald Duffy, Michigan State University

2. When the only vowel in a word or accented syllable is at the end of the word or accented syllable, it has a long sound.

   Examples: ba con   me   Bi ble   no   pu pil

3. When the only vowel in a word or accented syllable is followed by r or w, the sound of the vowel is usually controlled. The letter 1 can also control the vowel a.

   Examples: party   paw   her   forest   now   always

4. In many words of more than one syllable, there is a diminished stress on one of the syllables. This diminished stress is referred to "as a softening of the vowel sound." It is called a schwa sound and is represented by the symbol that looks like an upside down e.

   Examples: bedlam   beaten   beautiful   beckon

5. When y is the only vowel in word or accented syllable, it has the sound of i. When y concludes a word of two or more syllables, it has the sound of long e.

   Examples: my   trying   baby   lady

6. When c is followed by e, i, or y, it has a soft sound (s).

   Examples: city   cent   since

   Letter g also has a soft sound in some words (j).

   Examples: judge   ginger

Rules for Two Vowels

1. When there are two adjacent vowels, each contributing to the sound heard (blending), they are called diphthongs. The diphthongs are ou, ow, oi, oy.

   Examples: house   owl   oil   boy

2. When there are two vowels together in a word or accented syllable, usually the first has a long sound (says its name) and the second its silent. "When two vowels go a-walking the first one does the talking."

42

Such vowel combinations are sometimes called "vowel digraphs."

Examples: beat   fea ture   east   beat ing

3. When there are two vowels in a word or accented syllable, and one of them is final e (silent e), the first vowel usually says its name - is long - and the final e is silent.

    Examples: ride   ice   fire   ode   place

4. When there is a single vowel followed by two consonants and final e, the vowel is usually short.

    Examples: chance   prince   pulse   twelve   else

5. The sounds of oo may be either long or short.

    Long oo: boo   cool   food   room   tough
    Short oo: book   foot   good   stood   wood

SYLLABICATION

Every syllable in our language contains a VOWEL SOUND.

Closed syllable - one which ends with a consonant. The vowel in a closed syllable is usually short.

    Examples: gob ble   sit   pic ture

Open syllable - the first syllable ending in a vowel. The vowel in this syllable is usually long.

    Examples: ta ble   ba con   ti ger

Rules for syllabication

1. When a word contains a double consonant, the division comes between these double letters. Examples: yel ow but ter

2. When two different consonants come between two vowels, the division usually comes between the consonants.

    Examples: don key   blan ket   har bor

3. When a single consonant comes between two vowels, the consonant usually goes with the second vowel. Examples: be gan   la pel

4. When words contain prefixes or suffixes, the prefix or
    suffix usually forms a separate syllable.
    Inflectional endings often come under this rule.

    Examples: ex cuse   slow ly   go ing   part ed

5. When a word ends in le, the consonant immediately
    preceding the le usually begins the last syllable.

    Examples: ta ble   jum ble   la dle

6. Compound words are divided between their word parts
    and elsewhere if a word part has two or more
    syllables.

    Examples: ranch man   base ball   mo tor boat
               ant eat er

7. Consonant blends and digraphs are considered as single
    consonants when words are divided into syllables.

    Examples: a phid   con gress   chick en   min strel

8. When the letter x ix preceded and followed by a vowel,
    it usually goes with the first vowel.

    Examples: Tex as   ex ile

9. When ed is preceded by d or t, it forms a separate
    syllable.

    Examples: start ed   strand ed

In words of two or more syllables, one syllable is stressed or
accented more than the others. ACCENT AFFECTS VOWEL SOUNDS IN
SYLLABLES. The vowel in the accented syllable usually has the
sound that can be expected. The vowel in the unaccented
syllable may not have the sound that might be expected,
substituting a schwa sound instead.

Rules for Accent

One accent - two syllables:
1. When the last syllable ends in a consonant followed by
    y, the first syllable is accented.

    Examples: la' dy   fif'ty

2. If the final syllable ends in le, the final syllable is usually unaccented.

    Examples: cra'dle   jum'ble

3. Prefixes, suffixes, endings that form separate syllables are usually unaccented.

    Examples: un lock'   read'ing   hope'ful

4. In inflected or derived forms, the accent usually falls on or within the root word.

    Examples: farm'er   jump'ing

5. If tion or ture is the final syllable it is unaccented.

    Examples: pic'ture   fea'ture

6. When the first vowel in a word is followed by two consonants, the first syllable is usually accented.

    Examples: jun' ket   grif' fin   gos' sip   cur' few

NOTE: In most words of two syllables, the first syllable is accented.

One Accent - more than two syllables.
The accent falls on the first or second syllable.

    Examples: de fer'ing   dom' i nate   le vi'a than

Two accents - strong - primary   light - secondary

1. Each part of a compound word has an accent. The primary accent usually comes before the secondary.

    Examples: run' way   mail'man

2. In words that are not compound words, the secondary accent frequently comes before the primary. The secondary will come on the first or second syllable.

    Examples: in' ca pac' i tate   per'son al'i ty

45

3. There is usually one unaccented syllable between the syllable with the primary and secondary accents.

    Examples: rep' re sent'   trans' por ta' tion

Comprehension Skills

The importance of skill in recognizing words has just been pointed out to you. While it is not possible for a person to read without being able to recognize words, word recognition does not constitute all of reading. It is merely a tool for reading. In order for the child to become an effective reader, he/she must be able to comprehend what is read. Reading with comprehension means that the child is able to get meaning from what is being perceived in writing. There is controversy among leaders in the field of reading regarding whether or not reading comprehension is a general ability or a combination of various skills. The position taken here is that reading comprehension involves the development of several specific skills, and that improvement in one comprehension skill does not necessarily result in improvement in others. The following specific comprehension skills are identified by Dallmann, Rouch, Chang, and DeBoer (1974), and in the view of this writer, need attention as the classroom teacher plans reading instruction:

1. Reading to find the main idea - The child reads fiction and other types of reading to get the general idea of a selection. The child reads to find what the general topic is or what the main idea of a selection might be.

2. Reading to select significant details - The child reads to recall specific facts that are included in the selection. He/she is able to tell how many days it took to cross the prairie or how many buttons there were on the general's coat.

3. Reading to follow directions - The child reads a selection, and upon finishing, is able to put something together or do something.

4. Reading to answer questions - Reading to find the answer to one or more questions is one of the common goals for reading in the elementary school. Often, the questions are asked by the teacher. However, boys and girls also need to develop the ability to formulate questions for themselves.

5. Reading to summarize and organize - The child must be able to read and to sense the relationship between the main point and the details, as well as the relationship among the details.

6. Reading to arrive at generalizations - To arrive at generalizations, the reader needs to note specific instances and then decide whether the data presented are sufficient to warrant a significant conclusion.

7. Reading to predict outcomes - Skill in predicting outcomes is useful in helping the reader note when he/she has misread a word or a group of words in a sentence. It is also of value because the person who is adept at predicting outcomes can usually get the thought more quickly than the others.

8. Reading to evaluate critically - In reading critically, the reader needs to learn to ask questions such as: Is the material relevant? Is the author qualified to discuss the subject? Does the author draw valid conclusions?

9. Reading to get meaning from phrases, sentences, and longer selections - Getting meaning from or through the printed page involves the ability to perceive and understand words in relationship to other words. The reader needs experiences in getting meaning from material of varying length and subject matter.

IV. Evaluation:

On "YOUR OWN PAPER" page 181, answer the following questions. When you finish, check your work with the KEY found in Appendix H page 135. Assign 5 points to each question you answer correctly.

1 - 4 . . . Identify four word recognition skill techniques that are needed by children as they become effective readers.

5 - 10. . . Identify six specific comprehension skills that need development with children as they become effective readers.

11 . . . Which of the following words contains a schwa sound?
(a) beautiful   (b) ginger   (c) baby   (d) house

12 . . . Which of the following is not a consonant digraph?
(a) cl   (b) ph   (c) kn   (d) ch

47

13   . . . Which of the following words contains an open
          syllable?
          (a) bacon   (b) gobble   (c) saddle   (d) puncture

14 - 20 . . Directions: Read each item carefully. Select the
                          letter or word which does not belong.
                          Mark your choice on your answer paper.

14. bed, bad, bill, bile, bug:

     a) bill, because it is the only one with a double l
     b) bile, because it contains a long vowel among words
         with a short vowel
     c) bile, because it is the only one ending with e
     d) bad, because it contains a diphthong

15. ai, oa, oy, ee

     a) oa, because it is a diphthong among blends
     b) ee, because it is a digraph double letter
     c) ai, because the i is usually silent and the other
         letters are all sounded

16. sp, spr, sh, sw
     a) sp, because it is a blend among digraphs
     b) spr, because it has three letters
     c) sh, because it is a digraph among blends
     d) sw, becaue it is a digraph among consonants

17. rain, mane, rat, reign
     a) rain, because it is the only one with a diphthong
     b) mane, because it is the only one with a silent letter
     c) rat, because it is the only one with a short vowel
         sound
     d) reign, because it is a monograph

18. then, those, think, the
     a) then, because it is the only word with a voiceless th
     b) those, because it is the only word with a voiced th
     c) think, because it is the only word with a voiced th
     d) think, because it is the only word with a voiceless th

19. in, sub, ism, re
     a) sub, because it is the only whole word in the group
     b) sub, because it is the only prefix in the group
     c) ism, because it is the only suffix in the group
     d) sub, because it is the only derivative in the group

20. l, y, m, n, t
    a)   l, because it is sometimes a vowel
    b)   t, because it has an explosive sound
    c)   y, because it is sometimes a vowel
    d)   m, because it can never form a blend

B. If you do not achieve a score of at least 90%, you may want
    to re-read portions of this chapter.

"Having a knowledge of the variety of approaches available will enable the teacher to match the child with an approach that seems to bring success."

5

Various Approaches

to Reading

Instruction

CHAPTER FIVE: Various Approaches to Reading Instruction

I. Directions for study of the chapter:

    A. Read the list of competencies to be developed in the chapter.

    B. Complete the pre-assessment activities to help you set purposes for your reading.

    C. Check your pre-assessment work with the appropriate key in the appendices.

    D. Complete the reading activity.

    E. Complete the evaluation for the chapter and check your work with the appropriate key in the appendices.

II. Competencies to be developed:

Upon completion of this chapter, the reader will be able to:

    A. Characterize the Basal Reader Approach to reading instruction.

    B. Characterize the Phonics Approach to reading instruction.

    C. Characterize the Linguistic Approach to reading instruction.

    D. Characterize the Individualized Approach to reading instruction.

    E. Characterize the Language Experience Approach to reading instruction.

III. Pre-assessment: Complete your pre-assessment on "YOUR OWN PAPER" page 183. When you finish, check your work with the KEY found in Appendix I page 137.

    A. Identify one advantage of the Basal Reader Approach to reading instruction.

    B. What is the best approach to reading instruction in the elementary school classroom?

C. (Answer True or False) - - - Phonic programs in reading instruction emphasize concern for the development of comprehension skills.

D. Briefly describe what is meant by the term "linguistics."

E. Identify one disadvantage of the individualized approach to reading instruction.

F. What is the term used to describe the approach to reading instruction in which the language patterns of reading materials are determined by a child's oral language?

IV. Reading Activity:

Since, in the democratic classroom thus far discussed, the teacher strives to provide individual learning alternatives for all children, at all levels of growth and development, it is important that the classroom teacher has at least a basic knowledge of the variety of approaches to reading instruction that are available for use as learning alternatives are provided. Often a child may not respond to a particular approach. Having a knowledge of the variety of approaches available will enable the teacher to match the child with an approach that seems to bring success. While there are several approaches, materials, techniques, and programs available to teachers today, only a few that have implications for the elementary classroom have been selected for treatment here. As you examine the basic characteristics of the approaches, you might want to keep in mind the following statement made by Robert Dykstra and cited in Dallmann, Rouch, Chang and DeBoer (1974):

> . . . The superiority of a single method of reading instruction is yet to be determined. It appears that a composite of methods would produce the best results and that an effort should be made to determine what each method would contribute to the reading program (pp. 489-490).

The intent here is to help you characterize the following approaches to reading instruction: Basal Reader Approach, Phonic Approach, Linguistic Approach, Individualized Approach, and Language Experience Approach.

Basal Reader Approach

When the teacher utilizes a basal reader approach, he/she uses a series of books and accompanying materials that are preplanned, sequentially organized, and designed to help the child learn the skills of developmental reading. Typically, such a series starts with one or more readiness books, usually in workbook form. The first normal reading materials are usually a series of thin paperbacks that are called pre-primers. Instead of being arranged by grade levels, the materials are often organized in such a way that several books may actually be used at a particular grade level. Workbooks usually accompany textbooks at each level, and teacher's manuals are also furnished for the teacher.

As the teacher uses a basal reader approach, he/she usually prepares the children for their reading by arousing their interest, teaching and clarifying ideas, concepts, and meanings that may be unfamiliar to some of the children, and then teaching them about new words that may be encountered in the reading assignment. The teacher follows this by discussing the title, silent reading, oral reading, and then discussion. Lessons are often concluded by having the children participate in some follow-up activity involving skills development and/or enrichment activities.

The following are some of the possible advantages of the basal reader approach:

1. The stories can provide a common center of interest with a group of children.

2. The skills program is carefully structured, systematic, and sequential.

3. Teacher's guides are usually well organized and can save much teacher planning time.

The following are some of the possible disadvantages of the basal reader approach:

1. The stories are often artificial, stilted, monotonous, and unduly repetitious.

2. Vocabulary is sometimes "over-controlled."

3. The use of basal materials often causes the teacher to get into a "rut" in his/her teaching of reading.

Phonic Approach

An examination of literature on the phonic approach to reading instruction indicates that most formal phonics programs emphasize the pronunciation or decoding aspects of beginning reading. Proponents of such an approach indicate that children will learn to comprehend what they read after they can "break the code." Therefore, phonic programs do not seem to include much concern for comprehension development. According to Miller (1977):

> The authors of formal phonics programs usually recommend that the program be presented to all children in a class, whether or not they have good auditory discrimination (the ability to hear the similarities and differences in sounds) and the required mental age to succeed in the program. They apparently believe that their program is the one best way of teaching beginning reading skills to all children in kindergarten or first grade and to all severely disabled readers (p. 101).

In many cases, formal phonics programs are total or basic and indicate that a phonics approach should be taken to the entire reading program in a classroom with the exception of independent trade book reading.

Formal phonics programs differ in the order of presentation of the various phonic analysis skills. In some programs the short or long vowel sounds are presented before the consonant sounds. Usually, however, the consonant sounds are presented first in formal phonics instruction.

Many of the current phonics basal reader programs contain soft covered books, workbooks, and audio visual aids such as filmstrips, cassette tapes, or video screens. Supplementary formal phonics programs often consist of charts, soft-covered books, workbooks, and audio visual aids.

In general, recent phonics basal reader programs take the more conventional basal reader format but start with a heavy emphasis on teaching symbol-sound associations. This is followed by instruction in blending the sounds into words and then introduction of meaningful context. Phonic programs have in common a stress on word recognition through the learning of the phonemic equivalents of letters and letter groups and the application of the phonetic and structural analysis generalizations previously discussed in this chapter.

One advantage of using the phonic approach is that it tends to stress the decoding process. Disadvantages include that it over-emphasizes a single word analysis skill and also that such an approach tends to neglect reading for meaning.

Linguistic Approach

Linguistics has been defined in many ways. It has been defined as the study of language. LeFevre has defined it as a scientific method of studying language. Those who have spent time studying the language have most often been individuals outside of the field of reading. However, they have had an impact on the approach many have developed for use in teaching children to read. Many linguists have expressed a critical attitude toward phonics teaching. They condemn phonics teaching on the grounds that such teaching typically proceeds from the sound to the word (synthetic approach) rather than from the word to the sound (analytic approach). They also charge that phonics instruction is poorly organized, that the sight method encourages guessing, and that it encourages word by word reading. In general, the linguists place much emphasis during the initial period of reading instruction on the importance of selecting words for mastery on the basis of the spelling pattern; not on frequency of use. They seem to agree that the aim of beginning instruction should be word recognition through the study of words with like spelling patterns such as can, nan, ban, and van. Some even advocate the inclusion of nonsense words in such instruction. Linguists emphasize the point that reading and writing are relatively recent inventions, and that they are derived from spoken language. They seem to regard the study of speech sounds as central to any defensible theory of reading instruction.

Since the publication of Leonard Bloomfield's work in 1961, several reading series based on linguistic principles have appeared on the market. They have in common agreement that "decoding is the most important goal of a reading program." Although linguistic readers are designed primarily for initial reading instruction, in some series the program extends through the second or third grades. After the completion of linguistic materials, children are expected to transfer to regular reading materials. Again, it needs to be emphasized that linguistic readers stress the controlled introduction of vocabulary guided by regular spelling patterns. In the linguistic approach, there is a heavy emphasis on decoding the print because many linguists claim that the child already knows the meaning of the words which he/she is decoding. Since several linguists feel that pictures encourage children to guess rather than to recognize printed word forms, pictures are most often omitted from linguistic readers except when they are used to make books more attractive. In this case, they are used but do not correlate with the story content.

The following are possible advantages of using a linguistic approach:

1. The approach stresses the decoding process and makes the child aware of sound symbol relationships.

2. The approach builds an awareness of the structure of the language.

The following are possible disadvantages of using a linguistic approach:

1. The approach often causes the teacher to neglect meaning.

2. The approach often results in the teacher neglecting the development of reading interests

Individualized Approach

Since about 1950, professional literature has given great attention to the individualized approach to reading instruction which stresses principles of child development in the implementation of an instructional reading program. It is important to note that individualized instruction and individualized reading are not synonymous. Individualizing instruction is basic to any effective teaching. The term individualized reading refers to a specific approach to formal reading instruction. According to Wilson and Hall (1972), the major characteristics of individualized reading are:

1. Pupils select their reading material from a wide variety of books available in their classroom and/or school library.

2. Each pupil reads different material and moves at his/her own pace through the material selected.

3. Direct instruction occurs in a pupil-teacher conference rather than in a reading group.

4. The reading materials are trade (library) books rather than basal readers (p. 64).

When the informal individualized approach is used, each child selects a book to read. The teacher usually schedules individual conferences with each child for about ten minutes. During part of this time, the child reads orally to the teacher. Careful records are kept on each child. In addition to asking questions about the reading, the child has done, the teacher usually helps the child with skill problems as they are revealed. Often, small groups are set up for skills instruction if several children are found to have similar skill needs.

The following are some of the possible advantages of the individualized approach to reading instruction:

1. The approach enables the teacher to meet individual differences in ability and interest.

2. The approach combines the best of recreational reading and one to one instruction.

3. The emphasis is on books children have selected.

The following are some of the possible disadvantages of the individualized approach:

1. The approach often makes it difficult for the teacher to evaluate and keep records.

2. Skill teaching is often done in a haphazard manner.

3. A large selection of books is needed.

Language Experience Approach

The language experience approach is often used as an approach to initial reading, to remedial reading, and as a supplement to other approaches. According to Wilson and Hall (1972), in this approach the language patterns of the reading materials are determined by a child's oral language, and the content of reading materials is determined by his/her experiences. These authors cite the following major characteristics of this approach:

1. The majority of reading material is pupil-produced.

2. The teaching of reading is integrated with instruction in the other language arts.

3. Vocabulary is not controlled since any words a child uses in his speech can be used in the reading materials (p. 60).

Although the language experience approach is most often used as an approach to beginning instruction, it is also used at other elementary school grade levels. Whenever it is used, the children are encouraged to express their thoughts, ideas, and feelings. These are often stimulated by a specific experience which is developed out of the oral language of the children, to a program of reading instruction which places an increasing emphasis upon a variety of children's books.

The following are some of the possible advantages of the language experience approach to reading instruction:

1. The approach helps to integrate language arts and reading instruction.

2. It helps the children tie spoken and written language together.

3. The approach helps the teacher meet individual differences in ability and interests.

Some of the possible disadvantages of the language experience approach as follows:

1. The approach involves a great deal of teacher work.

2. Skill teaching tends to become haphazard.

3. The approach lacks a specific sequence and system.

V. Evaluation:

A. On "YOUR OWN PAPER" page 185, answer the following questions. When you finish, check your work with the KEY found in Appendix J page 139. Assign 10 points to each question you answer correctly. 1-5 List five approaches to reading instruction at the elementary school school level.

6   (Answer True or False) Phonic reading programs have in common a stress on word recognition skills.

7   (Answer True or False) One major advantage of the individualized approach to reading instruction is that it builds an awareness of the formal structure of our language.

8   (Answer True or False) One characteristic of the basal reader approach is that direct instruction occurs in a

60

pupil-teacher conference rather than in a reading group.

9   (Answer True or False) The individualized approach to reading instruction combines the best of recreational reading and one to one instruction.

10 (Answer True or False) When the language experience approach to reading instruction is used, vocabulary is not controlled.

B. If you do not achieve a score of at least 90%, you may want to re-read portions of the chapter.

"Through careful lesson planning, reading activities can be integrated with other language arts activities."

6

<u>Planning Reading</u>

<u>Lessons</u>

CHAPTER SIX: Planning Reading Lessons

I.   Directions for the study of the chapter:

A.   Read the list of competencies to be developed in the chapter.

B.   Complete the pre-assessment activities to help you set purposes for your reading.

C.   Check your pre-assessment work with the appropriate key in the appendices.

D.   Complete the reading activity.

E.   Complete the evaluation for the chapter and check your work with the appropriate key in the appendices.

II.   Competencies to be developed:

Upon completion of this chapter, the reader will be able to:

A.   Identify the parts of a lesson plan that can be used in planning individual and group reading lessons.

B.   Identify at least two important "guidelines" for lesson planning in reading.

III.   Pre-Assessment: Complete your pre-assessment on "YOUR OWN PAPER" page 187.   When you finish, check your work with the KEY found in Appendix K page 141.

A.   Which of the following is a behavioral objective?

1.   Children will be able to understand how to spell the word "cat".

2.   Children will be able to spell the word "cat" correctly in written form.

B.   List, in order, the parts of a lesson plan you would follow if you were preparing to teach a reading lesson to a small group of fifth grade children.

IV. Reading Activity:

While it is important in all classrooms, efficient planning is especially important in the classroom where the emphasis is on freedom of movement for children, use of learning centers, pupil-teacher planning, individualization of instruction through learning options provided in the classroom environment, and flexibility in scheduling of daily learning activities. In order to have an effective reading program in such a classroom, the teacher needs to be very competent in planning; including lesson planning. It needs to be pointed out, however, that planning does not insure, but instead, facilitates, good teaching. While plans are not always written, such written plans are an exercise in orderly thinking about what is to be taught to a given group of children or an individual child in a specific teaching-learning situation. The beginning teacher should plan to write lesson plans until a pattern is firmly established regarding instructional planning. Written practice will help the beginning teacher develop a strategy for approaching the various teaching learning situations in the classroom. The following format is recommended for use in such plans:

Objectives

This is the part of the lesson plan in which the teacher identifies the objectives which he/she hopes to meet as a lesson is revealed to children. The good lesson usually will have few objectives; perhaps one to four. When only a few objectives are identified, the teacher can focus learning better than when too much is trying to be accomplished. The objectives should be written in behavioral terms. This means that they are stated in terms of what the children will be able to "do" as a result of instruction. The following are examples of behaviorally stated objectives:

1. At the conclusion of the lesson, the children will be able to:

   a) Identify, in writing, three main ideas in the story Mr. Putt Goes to Washington.

   b) Spell correctly, three words containing the vowel consonant final e pattern in words.

   c) Retell, in writing, the story Mr. Putt Goes to Washington in proper sequence.

65

You probably noticed that the preceding objectives are very specific and are, in fact, stated in terms of how children should be expected to behave as a result of the reading instruction. When objectives are specific, it is clear to the teacher that children will behave in a certain way if instruction is successful.

Materials

There is a clear indication that the teacher will probably need to use a variety of materials as he/she helps children learn to read. However, this will only really happen when the teacher plans to use a variety of materials. In this part of the lesson plan, the teacher indicates the specific materials and equipment he/she plans to use including the titles of specific films or filmstrips, the titles of specific cassettes, the pictures, art materials, etc. All materials that the teacher plans to use in the lesson should be listed in this part of the lesson plan.

Introduction and Motivation

This is the part of the lesson plan in which the teacher explains how he/she plans to introduce the lesson and motivate the children for the reading lesson. The teacher should strive to employ a variety of motivational techniques such as those discussed early in this handbook. Chances of learning taking place will be enhanced when the teacher gets the children interested in the lesson. Time needs to be spent planning the various ways this can be accomplished in a given lesson.

Procedure

This is the part of the lesson plan in which the teacher explains, step by step, how he/she plans to provide for individual differences, pupil participation, the principle of transfer, the principle of association, and the principle of effect. This is the part of the plan which might become an actual outline of how the teacher plans to proceed through the lesson once it has been introduced and the children have been motivated. In the early stages of teaching the teacher might actually refer to this part of the plan as the lesson unfolds with the children.

Evaluation

This is the part of the plan in which the teacher explains the means that will be used to determine whether or not the children learned what he/she wanted them to learn. The teacher strives to have consistency between the behavioral objectives and the evaluation. In addition, he/she should strive to employ a variety of evaluative techniques such as paper and pencil tests, discussion, games, and self evaluation.

The preceding lesson plan format should be helpful to the beginning teacher faced with planning reading instruction for children. The same strategy needs to be followed with a group or an individual child. As such planning is done, the teacher should keep the following "guidelines" in mind regarding lesson plan construction:

1. Written plans are important in terms of training the mind to think a lesson through before it is taught. As experience increases, the teacher usually can move away from the formal lesson plan. However, all lessons must be planned.

2. Time spent planning good lessons might be more valuable than time spent on clerical duties.

3. Lesson plans should be developed with consistency between objectives and evaluation.

4. Lesson plans should be developed with a view to planning lessons that will employ the principles of learning previously discussed in this handbook.

5. The classroom teacher needs to organize his/her teaching day in such a way that a sufficient amount of planning can actually take place in the classroom during work periods and free periods. This enables the teacher to plan in an environment in which all necessary resources are at hand.

6. While lesson plans are written with specificity, the teacher needs to be flexible in their use, so they can be adjusted to fit the last-minute needs of the day and the children for whom they were designed.

7. Lesson plans should be developed in reference to the teacher's manual of the textbook series. The persons making suggestions in the teacher's manual don't know your children. You do, and you should plan for them based upon

your knowledge of their abilities, weaknesses, and interests. This may often mean that you will choose to reject ideas presented in the teacher's manual.

8. An effort should be made to focus on specific skill development in the instructional part of the reading program. Therefore, plans should reflect concern for such skill development that can lead to more efficient and effective reading.

9. As plans are developed, the teacher may do well to plan activities related to strengths children have rather than to focus on those skills which need development. This can build security, self image, and interest in the instructional reading activities in the classroom. Few of us enjoy working on only those things we don't do well. Children can also feel this way. Efficient planning can provide the incentive that can lead up to reading improvement through building on strengths while correcting weaknesses.

10. Through careful lesson planning, reading activities can be integrated with other language arts activities. This can enhance chances of children seeing reading as one of the various communication processes available to them in daily life.

In order to improve your understanding of lesson planning as discussed thus far, you may find value in closely examining the following sample lesson plan. You will note that the sample plan reflects an effort to integrate reading with oral language, listening, handwriting, and composition skills. In addition the plan reflects a concern for specific skill development, the principles of learning, and consistency between stated objectives and the means of lesson evaluation.

SAMPLE LESSON PLAN

Prepared by: Robert C. Putt
                Associate Professor
                Department of Elementary Education
                Mansfield University

When Prepared: During class work sessions with students

Topic: Reading and Listening to Predict Outcome: A Total
          Communication Experience

1. Objectives
    At the conclusion of the lesson, the pupils will be able
    to:

    A. Read to predict the plot and eventual outcome of the
        story "The Railroad Cat" found on pages 6-13 of the
        reading text.

    B. Listen to predict the possible outcome of a story
        presented via audio tape by the teacher.

    C. Write an ending to a story dictated by the teacher via
        audio tape.

    D. Write cursively with uniformity of slant.

II. Materials

    A. Textbook - Around the Bend (Holt, Rinehart and
        Winston)

    B. Teacher's manual for Around the Bend

    C. Cassette tape recorder

    D. Cassette titled "A Day At The Horseheads Mall"

    E. Pictures of cat, dog, turtle, fish, and hamster

III. Introduction and Motivation

    A. Have pictures of the following pets in the chalk tray
        1. cat
        2. dog
        3. turtle
        4. fish
        5. hamster

    B. Ask children who have other pets to briefly describe
        them.

    C. Ask children to briefly discuss any of the animals
        which they have as pets.

    D. Ask the children if they have ever heard of heroic
        deeds pets have performed.

    E. Briefly allow children to discuss these deeds.

69

F.   Inform children that today we are going to read a story about a cat that performed an heroic deed.

G.   Ask children to take out their books and open to page 6.

H.   Ask children what they think is happening in the pictures on pages 6, 7, 8, 11, 12, and 13.

I.   Ask children to read first 9 pages silently to find out who Tom is and what he does that results in his being called "The Railroad Cat."

IV. Procedure

A.   Complete Motivation and Introduction

B.   Ask "What do you think will happen to Tom?"

C.   Provide children with time to orally discuss various possibilities.

D.   Ask children to finish reading the story silently for the purpose of determining what they predict might happen to Tom as he is locked in the box car.

E.   Remind children that, when they finish reading, they may work on anything that they find on the "When all is said and done bulletin board."

F.   Discuss the actual ending of the story.

G.   Set purposes for listening to the tape "A Day at the Horseheads Mall" (Listen to story and try to determine what you think may be the outcome of the story).

H.   Play tape, "A Day at the Horseheads Mall."

I.   Stop tape and ask children to predict the ending to the story.

J.   Ask children to discuss possible endings.

K.   Ask children to take out paper and write ending to story with attention to uniformity of slant.

V.   Evaluation

    A.   The teacher will observe to determine how many children can predict outcomes.

    B.   The teacher will collect written endings to stories to subjectively determine how many children were able to predict an outcome.

    C.   The teacher will check papers to determine whether or not children were able to write cursively with attention to uniformity of slant.

VI.   Evaluation:

    A.   Select a story from a basal reader and compose a written lesson plan for a specific group of children. Use "YOUR OWN PAPER" pages 189 and 191. Utilize the knowledge you gained from the chapter, and use the sample lesson plan as a model. When you finish, use the checklist found in Appendix L page 143 of this handbook to analyze your plan.

    B.   If you experience difficulty with this exercise, you may want to re-read portions of the chapter.

7

"The teacher needs to develop a classroom atmosphere in which children can "get the job done" and, at the same time, feel good about themselves and learning."

Classroom

Management

CHAPTER SEVEN: Classroom Management

I. Directions for study of the chapter:

A. Read the list of competencies to be developed in the chapter.

B. Complete the pre-assessment activities to help you set purposes for your reading.

C. Check your pre-assessment work with the appropriate key in the appendices.

D. Complete the reading activity.

E. Complete the evaluation for the chapter and check your work with the appropriate key in the appendices.

II. Competencies to be developed:

Upon completion of this chapter, the reader will be able to:

A. Identify at least five specific guidelines for classroom management.

B. Identify at least five specific guidelines for administering classroom discipline.

III. Pre-Assessment: Complete your pre-assessment on "YOUR OWN PAPER" page 193. When you finish, check your work with the KEY found in Appendix M page 145.

A. Identify three elements of classroom management, i.e., what are three aspects or areas of concern for the teacher as a classroom "manager."

B. Briefly describe the kind of discipline you think the teacher should strive to develop with children.

C. Briefly describe what you might do with a child who becomes "angered" or "irate" in class.

IV. Reading Activity:

Thus far in this handbook, there has been an obvious emphasis on the classroom atmosphere provided for children as they learn to read. While classroom management techniques are important in all areas of the daily program, it seems to this writer that this area is of particular importance as the teacher attempts to provide an atmosphere in which children can learn to read and can learn to enjoy reading as a communication process. Specifically, this means that the classroom teacher needs to be able to establish and maintain an appropriate informal classroom climate, maintain classroom control, and administer classroom discipline. The teacher needs to develop a classroom atmosphere in which children can "get the job done" and at the same time feel good about themselves and learning. The techniques employed by the teacher to manage the classroom atmosphere can have a profound impact on how children feel about themselves and the reading activities they experience. It makes sense to build an atmosphere in which children can relax, one in which they can concentrate, and one in which they feel secure, and one in which they learn to respect the individual efforts of everyone in the classroom. Accomplishing this with children requires exceptional classroom management skills on the part of the teacher.

According to Johnson and Bany (1970):

Classroom management can be conceived as a distinct pattern of activities by which teachers establish and maintain conditions whereby individuals in the classroom can apply all their rational, creative talents to the challenge of educational tasks. It is the development of an effective classroom organization, and a predictable system of relationships. It involves selecting the method appropriate to the situation where problems arise which affect the functioning of the class organization. It is a vital aspect of teaching because intellectual vigor cannot prosper if children's energies are constantly diverted by organizational problems or ineffective group relationships. Examples of such problems may be distractions caused by uncooperative individuals, or by group needs to make adaptations to relieve frustrating conditions. While the essence of classroom management is establishing an effective cooperative classroom system, another crucial aspect is successfully handling the human behavior problems

75

which arise in any organized face-to-face work group. Frayed tempers, suppressed or open hostility, individual or group frustrations resulting from ineffectual handling of the human problems in the classroom all lower or destroy individual competence. Therefore classroom management involves much more than merely establishing a cooperative work group, satisfactory working conditions, and coordinating efforts toward predetermined objectives. Management activities include maintaining the system and restoring it when unresolved problems threaten group integration, or cause individuals to react in disruptive and non-productive ways (pp. 9-10).

The following specific guidelines are recommended to the classroom teacher as he/she works to organize and coordinate the willing efforts of children to achieve their own educational objectives, i.e., as the teacher demonstrates effective classroom management abilities.

1. Project enthusiasm in your teaching. You cannot expect children to be interested in your reading lessons or any lessons unless you as the teacher act interested.

2. Project security as you work with children. This security will help establish a secure "climate" throughout the classroom.

3. Establish guidelines for the class. See that they understand them and see that they understand the consequences of going beyond these guidelines.

4. Demonstrate fairness to the class in all that you do. Children are great imitators and tend to be fair to you and each other when they see you demonstrate fairness.

5. Provide for individual differences. This means that you need to provide opportunities for each child to make unique contributions to various classroom activities. You need to plan work so that the abilities of each member of the class are utilized, rather than the abilities of just a few who are gifted.

6. Study and reflect upon the "typical" characteristics of children at the grade level at which you are teaching. When you know the characteristics of the children, you will better be able to develop and maintain a learning climate appropriate for them.

7. Apply the principles of learning discussed in this chapter to your work with the class. When things go wrong, ask, "Was there a principle of learning that would have helped me avoid the situation?"

8. Identify leaders in the class and allow them to help keep the class to the task at hand. Very often, such children can serve as "peer teachers" to other children.

9. Make a "When all is said and done bulletin board" on which you place interesting assignments for those who finish required work early. The learning climate and your control over it will be improved when you have children constructively involved.

10. Plan your lessons so you don't leave "gaps" in your teaching. Such gaps can often cause you to lose control over a lesson or the learning climate within the classroom.

11. Establish a receptive class atmosphere. Effective classroom management often depends upon the teacher's ability to give attention to the needs and requests of children.

12. Organize materials and equipment for effective use by the children. The use of learning centers can help you organize materials and equipment in a way that cuts down on the confusion and noise that can often lead to control and discipline problems.

One area of classroom management that is most often a concern of the beginning teacher is discipline. When discipline is considered by the classroom teacher, it is usually interpreted as involving mutual respect, understanding, and a growing self-control on the part of the children. The emphasis in the classroom needs to be placed on self-discipline. In the informal learning environment, the children need to learn self-control, to make correct decisions, and to govern one's actions in ways that will promote the happiness and well-being of oneself and others. In general then, discipline in the classroom means guiding children toward self-discipline. This is not an easy task. It should be noted that discipline is as much of a concern in the democratic and informal classroom as it is in any classroom. Democracy and informality do not mean an excess of permissiveness or a lack of discipline. It is up to the teacher to manage the classroom and structure it in such a way that children learn to become self-disciplined members of a group.

The following recommended guidelines for discipline are intended to help the classroom teacher in the effort to maintain discipline in a way that will move the children slowly toward the self-discipline they will need as members of society:

1. When you face a discipline problem, solve it then, within the framework of the guidelines that have been established. You can help the child develop self-discipline by helping him/her "understand" the guidelines that have been established for all children in the class.

2. Handle your own "discipline problems" when at all possible. When you send a child out of the room or to someone else, you admit defeat to the whole class. The next time you face a discipline problem, you may find it to be overwhelming due to a lack of respect for your ability to handle discipline.

3. When a child becomes irate, don't "pick" on him/her. Separate the child from the class and proceed until he/she "cools off."

4. Don't try to become a "buddy" to children. A good "buddy" does not always make a good teacher.

5. Be friendly but firm with all children, both in and out of the classroom. This kind of consistency will often help the children discipline themselves to exhibit appropriate behavior.

6. Don't play favorites in class. Children are very observant of how you treat them compared to other children.

7. Don't make up last minute "punishments." Think out purposeful and realistic measures that you feel you can use to handle a variety of situations.

8. Don't fight aggression with aggression. Often a "spanking" only makes a child more of a problem in the future.

9. Vary the tone of your voice and the rate at which you speak to hold interest and avoid control and discipline problems. Unless you are interesting to listen to, you can expect children to become easily distracted. This distraction can often result in a discipline problem.

10. Study permanent records for clues to reasons for problem behavior. This can often help you structure the classroom atmosphere and learning activities in such a way to avoid potential discipline problems.

11. Listen to the problems of individuals and contribute to their solution. Such a procedure can contribute a great deal to teaching children how to solve their own problems.

12. Remember, you were once a child. As you think back to your own childhood and school experiences, you may grow to realize that misbehavior and deviancy from accepted school practices are to be expected when you work with children.

V. Evaluation:

   A. On "YOUR OWN PAPER" page 195, and answer the following questions. When you finish, check your work with the KEY found in Appendix N page 147. Assign 10 points to each item you answer correctly.

       1 - 5   Identify five specific guidelines for classroom management that were discussed in this chapter.

       6 - 10   Identify five specific guidelines for classroom discipline that were discussed in this chapter.

   B. If you do not receive a score of at least 90%, you may want to re-read portions of the chapter.

"One of the advantages of a democratic
or informal structure in a classroom is
that such a structure offers the teacher
unlimited opportunities to integrate
what is done in reading with the total
language arts program."

8

Integrating Reading

with the Total

Language Arts

Program

CHAPTER EIGHT: Integrating Reading with the Total Language Arts Program

I.   Directions for the study of the chapter:

     A.   Read the list of competencies to be developed in the chapter.

     B.   Complete the pre-assessment activities to help you set purposes for your reading.

     C.   Check your pre-assessment work with the appropriate key in the appendices.

     D.   Complete the reading activity

     E.   Complete the evaluation for the chapter and check your work with the appropriate key in the appendices.

II. Competencies to be developed:

     Upon completion of this chapter, the reader will be able to:

     A.   Identify at least five elements or subject areas in the language arts program.

     B.   Cite a least five activities that can be used with children to integrate reading with the total language arts program.

III. Pre-Assessment: Complete your pre-assessment on "YOUR OWN PAPER" page 197. When you finish, check your work with the KEY found in Appendix 0 page 149.

     A.   Reading is often considered to be one of the "subject areas" or "elements" of the total language arts program. List five other "subject areas" or "elements" that are usually a part of the total language arts program at the elementary school level.

     B.   List five activities that can be used to integrate reading with other areas of the language arts program.

     C.   Briefly define a learning station as it relates to the elementary school classroom.

     D.   According to current views on language arts, what is the foundation or basis for all language skill development?

IV. Reading Activity:

One of the advantages of a democratic or informal structure in a classroom is that such a structure offers the teacher unlimited opportunities to integrate what is done in reading with the total language arts program. This, of course, enables the teacher to offer learning activities that will tend to develop the total communication skills of children in an integrated rather than a fragmented manner. According to Hildreth, cited by Dechant (1964), reading is communication and a linguistic process. Dechant points out the implications of this concept of reading. The implications follow and deserve scrutiny by the classroom teacher as an attempt is made to integrate reading instruction with the total language arts program:

1. There is little point in teaching a child to read until he can use sentence language in conversation.

2. It is unsafe for the reading text to run any considerable distance ahead of the child's own oral language expression; otherwise he is virtually trying to learn a foreign language and valuable instructional time is lost.

3. Language training should accompany reading instruction every step of the way. A linguistic background for reading lessons should be continuously built at each stage of growth.

4. The child's comprehension of speech and his oral use of language should be checked frequently. Appraisal of the linguistic competency of all slow learners and language handicapped children should be a part of the diagnostic and remedial program.

5. Every reading lesson should be an extension of language and a means of developing the child's linguistic skills.

6. More oral work should be provided in teaching beginners and handicapped pupils.

7. Some of the effort expended in teaching slow learners by dint of drills and devices might better be expended in working on development in oral language and comprehension.

8. More attention should be paid to aural comprehension as a pre-requisite for beginning reading. Language work should include ample experience in listening with full comprehension (p. 93). In his discussion of "Reading and the Other Language Arts," Karlin (1975) indicates:

Listening, speaking, and writing activities can also be incorporated into developmental reading instruction. In group language-experience reading, children listen for important ideas and details and for sequential order. They decide whether what they hear tells the story as it should be, whether certain ideas and words convey the message they wish to impart. Children are encouraged to be careful and discriminating listeners, sorting, and sifting the relevant from the unimportant. In individual language-experience reading, children hear the stories that others have created not only to listen for the ideas they contain but also to discover the unique ways in which they are expressed.

To put it another way, listening skills are strengthened by purposeful activities. In both basal and individualized reading programs, children have reasons to listen to what others read and say. The discussions that are part of basal reading lessons revolve around specific questions and issues, to which members of the group respond. Children must listen carefully in order to participate in discussions and resolve the questions. Frequently children will refer to what they have read in order to support their responses; the other children will listen as they read excerpts. Then the listeners must decide whether what they have heard supports the ideas that have been offered. Children also tell about books they have read on their own. Perhaps, they might read selected portions for the other children to enjoy. Again, the audience listens for a purpose: to become acquainted with authors and books they have not read in order to decide if they too choose to read them.

The expression of ideas through speaking and writing is both a preliminary to and an outgrowth of reading experiences. There is no reason why children cannot express their own ideas and those of others if there is a need for doing so. Oral and written language skills development is fostered when children feel a need to talk or write. At times, the need is a practical one; at other times it is an outgrowth of emotional feelings. Basal reading programs provide ample opportunities for children to engage in both speaking and writing. What is more, children become committed to reading by having their interest and curiosity aroused through preparatory activities. They relate what they already know to the story and consider the purposes for which they might read. (The emphasis at this stage is on oral language.) After the children have completed their reading, both oral and written language activities may follow if they flow naturally from the reading: spontaneous or planned dramatics, play or poetry reading, debating, interviewing, reporting, letter writing, creative prose or poetry writing (pp. 160-161).

One effective way of organizing the learning environment in the classroom so that children are provided opportunities to integrate their reading with the total language arts program is to utilize learning stations. According to Carrillo (1976), the use of learning stations can also help the teacher individualize while still keeping the advantages of group work and cutting down somewhat on multiplicity of plans. Possibilities for using learning stations to integrate reading with other language arts are limited only by the creativity and planning ability of the teacher. In general, a learning station consists of a group of children working together at a well-defined task. The task can easily involve the integration of several areas of reading and other language arts as children work on such things as social studies and science projects. The location may be a group of desks, a table, a study carrel, or a spot on the floor in some corner of the room.

As much as possible, directions should be posed at a station and should be self directing for the children. All supplies needed for the integrated activity should be located there. The teacher should act as a resource person and give individual assistance after a general introduction of the the task to the group. A number of learning stations can be in operation at the same time, and children may, according to a plan, circulate as a group during the day or the week. Listening, reading, writing, and speaking experiences can be integrated in an organized way through the use of learning stations.

Another way to integrate reading with the total language arts program is through the regular use of instructional game activities. The skills which are practiced through participation in the following game activities can be helpful to

85

children as they relate to their total language experiences including reading. The game activities are among several suggested by Burns and Lowe (1966):

1. <u>Dictionary</u> - Guide words for a page in the dictionary are put on the chalkboard. Sides A and B try to write the words that would appear on that page. The side with the larger number of correct entries is declared the winner.

2. <u>Golden Treasure Box</u> - A gold covered box is maintained for contributions of new expressions for a familiar idea. The box is opened once a week and the new expressions are read at that time.

3. <u>Lively Word</u> - All the pupils go to the board. Without looking at anyone's work but his own, each pupil writes a lively word for the verb used by the teacher. Example, "I ran across the street," might call forth such words as raced, dashed, flew, and rushed.

4. <u>Sentence Bag</u> - The teacher writes 15 complete sentences and 15 incomplete sentences on 30 small pieces of sturdy paper. These are placed in a box. The pupils take turns in drawing and reading aloud. The pupils are to tell whether they drew a sentence or a fragment.

5. <u>Story Box</u> - A shoe box is nicely decorated and is labeled "Story Box." Whenever a pupil has a story that he wants to share with the class, he drops it into the box. The box is opened once per week and the stories are read at that time.

Tiedt and Tiedt (1967) have indicated that the following can be done by children following the reading of a story in an effort to have them extend their reading into other language experiences:

1. Write a reaction to points made by the author.

2. Write a story suggested by the content.

3. Write poetry based on an idea.

4. Discuss unusual uses of words.

5. Study a specific sentence structure found in the story.

6. Enact a portion of dialogue.

In summary, there are several specific things the classroom teacher can do to integrate reading instruction with the total language arts program. In reference to the preceding discussion, some of the major ones are as follows:

1. Have children listen to stories to determine important ideas or sequence.

2. Have children use their speaking skills to tell about what they have read.

3. Have children write their reactions to what they have read. Handwriting and spelling can also be emphasized.

4. Have children dramatize stories that have been read. Speaking skills already learned can be practiced in this way.

5. Have upper grade children orally debate issues related to what they have read.

6. Have children use letter writing skills as they write reactions to what they have read. Handwriting and spelling can also be emphasized.

7. Have children write poetry on some topic that arises in a reading lesson or have them relate what they have read to similar material in poetic form.

8. Utilize learning stations to organize total language arts experiences related to reading, social studies, and science lessons or projects.

9. Utilize a variety of game activities that will enable children to grow in reading through their experiences in total language activities.

10. Have children use speaking skills to discuss unusual uses of words found in stories.

11. Have children orally discuss specific sentence structure found in stories.

V. Evaluation

On "YOUR OWN PAPER" page 199, answer the following questions. When you finish, check your work with the KEY found in Appendix P page 151 of this chapter. Assign 10 points to each question you answer correctly.

1. There is little point in teaching a child to read until he/she can use sentence language in conversation. (True or False)

2. Some of the effort expended in teaching slow learners by dint of drills and devices might better be expended in working on development in expressive written language. (True or False)

3. Oral and written language skills development is only fostered when the proper commercially prepared materials are used by the teacher. (True or False)

4. When using a learning station to integrate reading with total language arts instruction, the teacher should be at the station to give direct instruction. (True or False)

5. In order to utilize learning stations in the open classroom, the teacher must have access to study carrels. (True or False)

6-10. Identify five specific ways the open classroom teacher can integrate reading instruction with total language arts instruction.

9

"It is the view of this writer that the classroom teacher should take a diagnostic approach to reading instruction and that the diagnosis should include utilization of both standardized and informal instruments."

Diagnosis:

Developing a

Blueprint For

Instruction

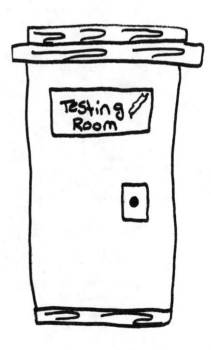

CHAPTER NINE: Diagnosis - Developing a Blueprint for Instruction

I.   Directions for study of the chapter:

   A.   Read the list of competencies to be developed in the chapter.

   B.   Complete the pre-assessment activities to help you set purposes for your reading.

   C.   Check your pre-assessment work with the appropriate key in the appendices.

   D.   Complete the reading activity.

   E.   Complete the evaluation for the chapter and check your work with the appropriate key in the appendices.

II. Competencies to be developed:

   Upon completion of this chapter, the reader will be able to:

   A.   Identify steps that could be taken to implement a diagnostic approach to classroom reading instruction.

   B.   Compute reading expectancy using the Bond Expectancy Formula.

   C.   Discuss the use of an informal reading inventory to determine the instructional, independent, and frustration reading levels for elementary and secondary level children.

III. Pre-Assessment: Complete your pre-assessment on "YOUR OWN PAPER" page 201. When you finish, check your work with the KEY found in Appendix Q page 153.

   A.   List the first 3 steps you would follow if you were to initiate a diagnostic approach to reading instruction in an intermediate grade classroom.

   B.   Name one test that could be used by the classroom teacher to determine the approximate intelligence quotient of children in the elementary and secondary school.

C.   Name a reading test that could be used to determine
the instructional reading level, frustration level,
and independent reading level for children at the
elementary and secondary school levels.

IV. Reading Activity:

Diagnosis

Classroom testing in reading has two purposes. One is
to diagnose pupils' needs. The other is to use these
results to provide a reading program based on those needs.
It seems to this writer that the second purpose is not
getting the attention it deserves.

While there are several problems to be confronted by
the teacher who takes a diagnostic approach to reading
instruction, one of the major ones the teacher faces is
that of test selection. Standardized group tests in
reading tend to overestimate pupil performance. For this
reason, they are often disregarded by classroom teachers
who rely entirely on informal measures to determine
instructional needs. The limitations of informal measures
have often been cited, i.e., lack of validity, lack of
reliability, and fragmentation of skill measurement.
Because of these limitations, some classroom teachers
hesitate to construct and use informal reading inventories.

It is the view of this writer that the classroom
teacher should take a diagnostic approach to reading
instruction and that the diagnosis should include
utilization of both standardized and informal instruments.
In addition, the results of the diagnosis should be
collated to provide the most complete group diagnosis
possible. The strategy recommended here is one that is
time consuming. In most cases, it will require that, for
the first month of school, the teacher will need to have
only recreational reading while individual tests are
administered. During the first month, children can enjoy
the recreational aspect of reading while the teacher
uncovers the needs that are to be met within the
instructional program during the remainder of the school
year. The use of the strategy usually means that children
will not be placed in instructional reading groups until
the second month of school. However, at the beginning of
the second month, the teacher can know the needs of
children with precision and can place children in
appropriate materials within the classroom grouping scheme.
The strategy can be used with a variety of instruments

91

which might be available in a particular school. In order
to enhance the clarity of the strategy here, sample
specific tests have been cited. The teacher in a specific
classroom situation should feel free to substitute tests as
the strategy is modified for actual classroom use. It is
recommended that the classroom teacher utilize the
following strategy as a diagnostic approach to reading is
implemented:

1. Obtain an Intelligence Quotient

    Any use of IQ scores seems to be controversial.
    However, intelligence is an accepted factor that
    influences reading achievement. The score is needed
    in order for the teacher to compute reading expectancy
    later in this strategy. Often results of an
    individual intelligence test such as the Stanford
    Binet or the Wechsler Intelligence Scale for Children
    can be found in a child's cumulative folder. When
    such results that are not more than 1 year old can be
    found, the teacher would not need to administer an
    intelligence test. The teacher should be careful when
    intelligence is measured with children suspected of
    having serious reading difficulty. Such children
    should be given a nonverbal test in which the
    intelligence quotient is not dependent upon reading
    ability. A folder should be organized for each child,
    and the intelligence quotient can be recorded in each
    folder. The teacher will find the following
    instruments appropriate for use at the primary,
    intermediate, and secondary grade levels.

    Peabody Picture Vocabulary Test

    Slosson Intelligence Test for Children and
    Adults

2. Compute reading expectancy

    There are several ways in which the teacher can compute a
    child's potential or expectancy in reading. Such
    computational techniques have long been recognized and
    utilized by reading specialists. Once the expectancy level
    has been determined, the teacher will have a grade
    equivalent score with which to compare reading test scores.
    Without computed expectancy, the only thing the teacher can
    do is to compare test scores with grade placement. There
    is a notion held by some administrators and classroom
    teachers that suggests that a good reader is a child who is
    reading at the grade placement level. It might be more

appropriate to compare a child's reading achievement with computed expectancy so the teacher can better recognize the individual differences of children and give proper consideration to intelligence as a factor that affects reading growth. Once the expectancy score is computed, it can be recorded in each child's folder. Teachers at the primary, intermediate, and secondary levels might consider the use of the following Bond Expectancy Formula:

$$\text{Expectancy} = \frac{(\underline{\text{Intelligence Quotient}})}{100} \text{ X number of years in school} + 1.0$$

3. Administer a word recognition test

Too often, teachers administer reading achievement tests that are inappropriate for all children in a given classroom. When a test is appropriate for grades 3 – 9, chances are that the most reliable results will be obtained when only children who can recognize words at least at the grade 3 level are administered that specific test. Therefore, at all grade levels, the teacher should administer a short word recognition test prior to the achievement test in order to identify the level at which an individual child can recognize words. This word recognition score can be very helpful in helping the teacher to select the proper achievement test. The word recognition grade level score should be recorded in each child's folder. One instrument that the teacher might consider for use in obtaining a word recognition score is the reading portion of the Wide Range Achievement Test.

4. Administer a reading achievement test

It is important for the teacher to see how well a child can achieve in reading when compared to other children. This information can be achieved through the administration of an appropriate reading achievement test. Most achievement tests can be administered to the entire class at one time if all children can recognize words at the grade levels for which the particular achievement test is designed. In some cases, the teacher will find that some children cannot handle the words in the test taken by most of the group. In such cases, the teacher can find another achievement test for those children who need such consideration.

The results of the achievement test should be recorded in each child's folder. The following are sample specific instruments that the teacher might consider:

Primary level – <u>Gates-MacGinitie Reading Test</u> – Levels
R, A, and B, Forms 1 and 2

Intermediate level – <u>Nelson Reading Skills Test</u>, Forms
3 and 4

Secondary level – <u>Nelson Denny Reading Test</u>, Forms C
and D

5. <u>Administer an informal reading inventory</u>

While it is possible for classroom teachers to develop
their own informal reading inventories, there are also
commercially prepared ones that can be purchased for
classroom use. All informal reading inventories should
include individual administration and an oral reading
passage that will enable the teacher to hear each child
read. As errors are made during oral reading, they should
be recorded for later reference. The results of the
informal reading inventory will reveal the grade level at
which the child should receive instruction, the independent
reading level, and the grade level at which the child
becomes frustrated in reading. These scores should be
recorded in each child's folder. The teacher will find the
<u>Classroom Reading Inventory</u> by Silvaroli appropriate for
use at the primary, intermediate, and secondary grade
levels.

6. <u>Analyze the errors made on tests</u>

While it is important for the teacher to know the instructional, independent, and frustration reading levels derived
from testing, it is also important for the teacher to
analyze the errors made on all tests. It is especially
important to analyze the errors made during oral reading on
the word recognition test and also during oral reading on
the informal reading inventory. The following checklist
can be completed on each child after oral reading and
placed in each child's folder.

THE INFORMAL READING INVENTORY - TEACHER WORKSHEET

Name _____ Age _____ Grade _____

Examiner _____ Date _____

Test information: Score   Type   Name of Test

    Intelligence _____   _____   _____

       Reading _____   _____   _____

                        _____   _____

                        _____   _____

ORAL READING CHECK LIST   Check One   Informal Reading
                                        Stories

                            Instructional _____
                  Yes No Independent _____
                            Frustration _____

Reads word-by-word   ___ ___   _____

Phrases inappropriately   ___ ___   _____

Reads through punctuation ___ ___   Comprehension

Excessive mispronunciations ___ ___
                            Good   Fair   Poor

Faulty Enunciation   ___ ___   ____   ____   ____

                            Comprehension Errors

Reads without expression   ___ ___   _____

Tense or nervous   ___ ___   _____

Excessive repetitions   ___ ___   _____

Loses place   ___ ___   _____

Inadequate sight vocabulary ___ ___   _____

Guesses incorrectly from   ___ ___   _____
context

Inadequate sight vocabulary   ___ ___   _____

Reads slowly   ___ ___   _____

Skips words   ___ ___   _____

Adds words   ___ ___   _____

Reads too fast   ___ ___   _____

Does not try unknown words   ___ ___   _____

* Other comments can be made on the back of this form

In addition, the following error analysis form can be completed during all oral reading experiences and help the teacher categorize errors as future specific instruction is furnished.

ERROR ANALYSIS - TEACHER WORKSHEET

Name _____

Instructional Level _____

Independent Level _____

Error Analysis

I.   A.   Visual Perception - Enter words child said for what he
                              should have said. Make a
                              judgement regarding the part of
                              the word in which the error was
                              made. Example: fish/dish would
                              be entered in the column for
                              initial part of the word.

Initial	Medial	Final

     B.   Visual Perception - Syllabic Division: Enter here any
                              errors made that in your judgement
                              were due to difficulty with
                              syllabic division/ Example:
                              beautful/beautiful.

II. Visual Auditory Perception - Enter in the appropriate
                                  column errors that, in your
                                  judgement were due to specific
                                  difficulties with the various
                                  consonant and vowel sounds.
                                  Example: kahurch/ church
                                  would be entered under the
                                  column for consonant digraphs.

	Consonant Sounds			Vowel Sounds	
Single	Blend	Digraph	Single	Digraph	Diphthong

98

III. Structural Analysis   –   Enter here any errors that, in your judgement, were due to difficulty with prefixes, suffixes, inflectional endings, and compound words. Example: bordalk/boardwalk.

IV. Use the back of this sheet to note comprehension errors.

7.   <u>Collate the data collected on each child</u>

In addition to the steps outlined thus far, the teacher may want to obtain the results of a visual survey, obtain background information from parents, and administer an interest inventory. Once the teacher completes the diagnosis, it becomes important that the results be "pulled together" so the results can be used as a "blueprint" for instruction. The following form can be utilized as the teacher attempts to collate all data on each child. Completed forms can then be studied as grouping is determined and individualized instruction is planned.

Summary Diagnostic Form

Child's Name _____

Child's Age _____   Grade _____

Name of Clinician _____

1.   I.Q. Results _____   Date _____

2.   Informal Results _____   Date _____

    a)   Instructional Level _____
    b)   Independent Level _____
    c)   Frustration Level _____

3.   Computed Expectancy _____

4.   Standardized Test Given _____

5.   Results of Standardized Test   Date _____

    a)   <u>Vocabulary</u> – _____

    b)   <u>Paragraph</u> – _____

    c)   <u>Total</u> – _____

6.   Word Recognition Test Results _____ Date _____

7.   Visual Survey results _____

8.   What did interest inventory reveal? _____

_____

9.   What was the most important thing the parental interview

revealed? _____

10. What did the error analysis reveal? _____

_____

*   On the back of this form, make any other notes that will
     will be helpful as you build a blueprint for instruction with
     this child.

Following the completion of all steps in this strategy, the teacher can then begin to develop a tentative reading program that will provide experiences in instructional, independent, and recreational reading. As the program is developed, the teacher should also incorporate other pertinent knowledge that has been obtained through his/her observation of the children in the total classroom environment. In addition, as the teacher continues his/her interest and efforts toward developing a blueprint for instruction through the use of diagnostic procedures, he/she may find the following sources very helpful:

Bond, Guy L. Tinker, Miles A. and Wasson, Barbara B. Reading Difficulties: Their Diagnosis and Correction, 4th edition, Englewood Cliffs, N.J.: Prentice-Hall, 1979, Chapter 6, "Basic Considerations in Diagnosing Reading Difficulties," pp. 117-152.

Harris, A.J., and Sipay, E.R. How To Increase Reading Ability, 6 edition, New York: David McKay, 1975, Chapter 5, "Meeting Individual Needs in Reading," pp. 88-107.

Wilson, Robert, M. Diagnostic and Remedial Reading for Classroom and Clinic, 3rd edition, Columbus, Ohio: Merrill, 1977

V.   Evaluation:

On "YOUR OWN PAPER" page 203, number from 1-10 and answer the following questions. When you finish, check your work with the KEY found in Appendix R page 155. Assign 10 points to each question you answer correctly.

1-4. List the first 4 steps you would follow if you were to initiate a diagnostic approach to reading instruction in an intermediate grade classroom.

5-6. Name 2 tests that could be used by the classroom teacher to determine the approximate intelligence quotient of children in the elementary and secondary school.

7-9. List 3 reading levels that can be obtained through the administration of an informal reading inventory.

10. Name one commercially prepared informal reading inventory that could be used by a grade 3 classroom teacher who is using a diagnostic approach to reading.

10

"As material is selected for the corrective program, results of the informal inventory can be utilized to select material for the instructional, independent, and recreational activities."

Correction: Using

Diagnosis as a Blue-

print for Instruction

CHAPTER TEN: Correction - Using Diagnosis as a Blueprint
                for Instruction

I.   Directions for study of the chapter:

      A.   Read the list of competencies to be developed in the
            chapter.

      B.   Complete the pre-assessment activities to help you set
            purposes for your reading.

      C.   Check your pre-assessment work with the appropriate
            key in the appendices.

      D.   Complete the reading activity.

      E.   Complete the evaluation for the chapter and check your
            work the appropriate key in the appendices.

II.   Competencies to be developed:

      Upon completion of this chapter, the reader will be able
      to:

      A.   Cite at least five guidelines that the teacher should
            follow as corrective reading activities are provided
            in the classroom.

      B.   Characterize the specific elements of a classroom
            environment that will support success in corrective
            reading activities.

      C.   Suggest specific corrective reading activities that
            will help the teacher "treat" common classroom reading
            difficulties.

III. Pre-Assessment: Complete your pre-assessment on "YOUR OWN
      PAPER" page 205.   When you finish, check your work with the
      KEY found in Appendix S page 157.

      A.   List three guidelines that the teacher should follow
            as corrective reading activities are provided in the
            classroom.

      B.   List five elements of a classroom environment that are
            especially important for the support of corrective
            reading activities in the classroom.

      C.   Discuss one corrective reading activity that the

104

teacher could provide for children who seem to have an inadequate sight vocabulary.

D. Discuss one corrective reading activity that the teacher could provide for children who have difficulty reading to recall main ideas.

IV. Reading Activity:

As suggested in Chapter 9, the purpose of the reading diagnosis is to develop a blueprint for instruction. Unless the diagnosis serves this purpose, there is little or no value in having the teacher administer reading tests. The task ahead is to put the test results to work as the teacher builds a total reading program for the group and/or an in individual child. At the correction level, the teacher needs to utilize all data collected during the diagnosis to plan a program of reading instruction that will include instructional, independent, and recreational activities. As the teacher approaches this task, the following guidelines might be kept in mind:

1. Rather than plan activities to correct all deficiencies, the teacher should plan to attack one or two deficiencies at a time and continue to correct those deficiencies until mastery is evidenced.

2. Throughout the correction process, the teacher serves as a model. Therefore, the children should observe the teacher reading. This can be especially helpful as the teacher attempts to have the children practice their skills during independent and recreational reading. While the children are reading, the teacher should be reading.

3. The teacher needs to recognize that consideration of the children's interests is basic to success in corrective work. Therefore, the teacher should utilize data collected on an interest inventory to select materials that will be used with children in corrective reading activities.

4. During instructional activities, skills that have been found to be weak can be strengthened. However, it may be that the experiences that will give practice with such skills and that will, therefore, sustain the child throughout the school experience will take place during independent and recreational reading. This guideline suggests, therefore, that corrective work should involve instructional, independent, and recreational reading activities.

5.   As material is selected for the corrective program results of the informal inventory can be utilized to select material for the instructional, independent, and recreational activities. However, the material must be sufficiently easy to handle at the start to insure pupil success and satisfaction.

6.   Often children with reading problems are children with other problems involving self esteem. Therefore, the teacher needs to work to overcome children's feelings of defeat and inadequacy early in the corrective program.

7.   Children will often profit most from instructional activities that involve frequent short periods of practice that leave children desiring more.

8.   No one approach or material will guarantee improvement. Therefore, the teacher needs to keep an open mind regarding the use of various approaches and materials and should not hesitate to change the approach or material once it is found that a particular approach or material is not working.

9.   Often children will offer their own suggestions about what they would like to do during the reading period. The teacher should not hesitate to follow the valid suggestions of the children.

10. While the initial diagnosis can provide the teacher with much helpful data, the teacher should continue diagnosis throughout the entire period of corrective instruction and should adjust approaches and materials to maintain a challenge to the increasing competency of the children.

Attention to the guidelines suggested here will enhance the teacher's success in helping children correct their reading problems. Establishment of the proper classroom environment will also increase chances of success as children work to improve their reading abilities. Several suggestions have been given earlier in the handbook. When the proper environment has been established, the teacher should be able to answer "yes" to the following questions:

1.   Is there a library or reading corner which displays books in an enticing manner?

2. Does the reading corner provide a comfortable reading area in terms of chairs, table, and adequate lighting?

3. Is the classroom so arranged that the group working with the teacher is compact enough to enable all to hear without using a loud voice?

4. Is the classroom so arranged that the group working with the teacher is far enough from those working independently so that it is not disturbing to others?

5. Does the classroom contain displays of pupil language efforts to stimulate interest in the processes of communication?

6. Does the classroom have charts to guide the development of reading, listening, and speaking skills?

7. Does the classroom contain books of varying readability levels related to different topics and of diverse types?

8. Does the classroom contain an area for book reviews, book information, and pupil comments?

9. Does the classroom contain charts to reinforce word meanings and principles of word analysis?

10. Does the classroom contain a specific area in which children can display their own stories and exchange them for stories written by other children?

Once the teacher reflects upon the basic guidelines suggested here, and after the proper environment that will support corrective reading activities has been established, the teacher can then work with individuals and small groups to help children correct their difficulties. In an effort to help with this task, a few of the common difficulties that children seem to experience are treated below. The teacher may find it helpful to try some of the suggested corrective activities as he/she works with children who exhibit the selected difficulties. For more suggested corrective activities, the teacher might consult the following sources:

Bader, Lois A. Reading Diagnosis and Remediation in Classroom and Clinic. New York, New York: MacMillan Publishing Company, 1980, pp. 87-118.

Zintz, Miles, V. Corrective Reading. Dubuque, Iowa: Wm. C. Brown Company Publishers, 1981, pp. 223-283.

DIFFICULTY	SUGGESTED CORRECTIVE ACTIVITY
The child reads word by word in oral reading.	Have the child use a plain white card as a marker under his/her reading. This may improve the number of words seen during each stoppage of the eye. In addition, emphasize silent reading rather than oral reading and do not have such a child follow along silently while others read orally.
The child loses his/her place during oral reading.	Provide the child with a plain white card to use under words during silent and oral reading. Such a child may profit from instruction with the SRA controlled reading materials and/or other mechanically paced silent reading exercises.
The child does not seem to attempt to unlock unfamiliar words.	Such a child often has an over-emphasis on sight vocabulary and needs to receive instruction that will build confidence in the use of context clues, phonetic analysis, structural analysis, picture clues, and the use of the dictionary.
The child seems to depend on others to pronounce words during oral reading.	The child may lack confidence in the use of a variety of word recognition skill techniques. Pause and encourage child to unlock words. Have the child keep a log of words that are difficult to pronounce and use drill to put such words into the sight vocabulary.
The child repeats words often during oral reading.	This may indicate that the child is experiencing some regressions and/or other eye movement difficulty in silent reading. A plain white marker to follow with may help. Such eye movement difficulty may require experience

DIFFICULTY	SUGGESTED CORRECTIVE ACTIVITY
	with self paced, teacher paced, and mechanically paced reading activities.
The child substitutes other words during oral reading.	When such substitutions do not change meaning, it may not indicate any more than carelessness and a reminder may be all that is needed. However, when the meaning is changed by such behavior, the child may need silent and oral reading experiences which demand accurate interpretation. Such experiences could include oral reading of directions to be carried out by others.
The child does not seem to recognize words that should be in his/her sight vocabulary.	More drill may be needed on basic sight vocabulary. In order to motivate the child, place words on a plain card and assign monetary value to each card by placing that value on the back of each word card. When you flash words for child, he/or she keeps the cards with words correctly pronounced. The teacher keeps the cards for words missed. At the end of the activity, compute who won the most money in the game.
The child has trouble distinguishing between words that are similar in spelling such as "there" and "where."	In some cases, expanded work in sight vocabulary will help. Sometimes the child needs instruction in attacking words from left to right. In this case a marker may help. Exercises involving beginning sounds in words may help child pay closer attention to beginning sounds. Sometimes the child will be aided by tracing the letters in the words to note the differences in the words.

DIFFICULTY	SUGGESTED CORRECTIVE ACTIVITY
The child confuses "p" and "g", "was" and "saw" and seems to reverse other letters or words.	Children can trace the letters of words which have been written in large letters. In addition, the children can be encouraged to use a marker to move from left to right under lines of print.
The child does not seem to use context clues.	The cloze procedure can be an aid to help with all comprehension skills. It may be found to be especially useful in developing skill in the use of context clues. A passage should be written with every "nth" word missing with a blank of standard length substituted. For example, when every fifth word is left out, the child can read the passage and write in the missing words.
The child seems to read all material at a very slow pace.	The teacher should be sure to provide independent and recreational reading materials at a suitable readability level. Conduct timed reading exercises in material such as Reader's Digest Skill Builders. Make a tachistoscopic device out of 3 x 5 cards and allow reader to run it along a line of print to prevent regressions in eye movement.
The child reads too fast and does not seem to comprehend what has been read.	The teacher needs to emphasize reading for meaning. It usually helps to give the reader frequent comprehension questions before silent reading. Following silent reading, the reader should answer the questions in writing and keep a progress chart to have a record of results when careful reading for meaning is done.

DIFFICULTY	SUGGESTED CORRECTIVE ACTIVITY
The child projects a negative attitude and does not seem to like reading.	Be sure to provide recreational reading that is easy and that is about topics that will interest him/her. Have children keep progress charts so they can realize that the ability to read is improving. It sometimes helps to give children a list of particular difficulties which he/she should attempt to overcome. The teacher can also go to the library with children to help them select books at the proper readability level. It also helps when the teacher introduces children to new books in as interesting way as possible.
The child moves his/her lips while silent reading.	When a child does this, the teacher should be careful about having the child follow silently while others read orally. Too much oral reading can actually cause the behavior. Make the child aware of the behavior and remind him/her frequently when such behavior is exhibited. The teacher should also be careful not to exhibit such behavior in front of the children.
The child constantly selects reading material beyond his/her reading ability.	The child needs the teacher's help in book selection. The teacher can help the child examine a page in each of four sections of the book. If the child cannot recognize approximately 10 words per page, the child should be advised to select another book. The teacher may need to spend additional time helping the child uncover latent interests and readable material within various interest areas.

112

DIFFICULTY	SUGGESTED CORRECTIVE ACTIVITY
The child likes to be read to but does not seem to like to read.	Assign work that the child is interested in and require silent reading as a part of the task. Actually give the child selections to read that are attractive and suitable for his/her ability. It sometimes helps to have contests to see who can read the most books or stories in a specific length of time.
The child is unable to follow written directions.	Give the child written directions to do things around the room or the school building. This can often be done by writing a brief letter and giving it to a child at the beginning of the school day.
The child has difficulty recalling specific facts following silent reading.	Give the child riddles to solve. In addition, have the child or the children read a paragraph and answer fact questions in writing. Gradually increase the amount read before asking questions until a whole selection can be read. It usually helps to let children know, in advance, that specific questions about a selection will be asked following silent reading. Some children also respond well to completing a brief outline on material that is read.
The child has trouble recalling main ideas.	Give the child or a group of children construction paper divided into four equal sections. Following the reading of a selection, have the reader or readers draw four pictures that will depict the four main ideas of a selection. It usually helps to start with short selections for finding main ideas and to gradually increase the length of material read.

DIFFICULTY	SUGGESTED CORRECTIVE ACTIVITY

The child has difficulty
recalling sequence.

Children often respond to drawing to show the sequence of a story or book. Simple outlining activities can also help the child determine and retain the sequence of events in a story or book.

V. Evaluation:

A. On "YOUR OWN PAPER" page 207, answer the following questions. When you finish, check your work with the KEY found in Appendix T page 161. Assign 10 points to each question you answer correctly.

1-5. List five guidelines that should be followed as the teacher provides corrective reading activities in the classroom.

6-8. List two elements of a classroom environment that are especially important for the support of corrective reading activities in the classroom.

9. Identify one corrective activity that could be used with children who lose their place in oral reading.

10. Identify one corrective activity that could be used with children who have difficulty recalling specific facts following silent reading.

B. If you do not achieve a score of at least 90%, you may want to re-read portions of the chapter.

APPENDICES

A. While a variety of definitions may be acceptable, this author suggests that reading is a process of communication in which one person's ideas are exchanged with another person through the use of printed symbols.

B. Any three of the following skills represent a correct response:

    1. sight vocabulary development
    2. context clues
    3. phonetic analysis
    4. structural analysis
    5. reading to find main ideas
    6. reading to select significant details
    7. reading to follow directions
    8. reading to answer questions
    9. reading to summarize and organize
    10. reading to arrive at generalizations
    11. reading to evaluate critically
    12. reading to get meaning from phrases sentences, and longer selections

C. Any four of the following factors would represent an appropriate response:

    1. visual abilities
    2. auditory abilities
    3. oral language abilities
    4. general health
    5. intelligence
    6. personal and social adjustment
    7. home environment
    8. attitudes
    9. cultural and language differences
    10. readiness for beginning reading
    11. methods of teaching

D. The instructional part of the program is that part of the reading program through which the teacher provides children with the basic skills, attitudes, and appreciations in reading. The independent part of the reading program is the part of the program in which the child is encouraged to read without direct teacher assistance to answer questions or complete a particular task. The recreational reading part of the reading program is the part of the program in which the teacher encourages children to really enjoy reading, to explore present interests through reading, to delve into new interests, and to generally develop the habit of reading as a pleasurable activity.

A. 1-3 You should have included the following three in any
        order:

        Physical
        Decoding
        Thinking

    4-6 You should have included any three from the following
        list:

        sight vocabulary
        context clues
        phonetic analysis
        structural analysis
        reading to find main ideas
        reading to select significant details
        reading to follow directions
        reading to answer questions
        reading to summarize and organize
        reading to arrive at generalizations
        reading to evaluate critically
        reading to get meaning from phrases, sentences, and
            larger selections

    7-9 You should have included any two factors from the
        following list:

        visual abilities
        auditory abilities
        oral language abilities
        general health
        intelligence
        personal and social adjustment
        home environment
        attitudes
        cultural and language differences
        readiness for beginning reading
        methods of teaching

    10. The correct response is the independent reading level.

B. If you do not achieve a score of at least 90%, you may want
    to re-read portions of the chapter.

A. While there are many characteristics that could be cited, any five from the following list would be most appropriate for our purposes in this chapter:

1. freedom of movement for children
2. use of learning centers
3. pupil-teacher planning
4. individualization of instruction
5. flexibility in scheduling
6. open ended learning opportunities

B. While there are several typical freedoms and corresponding responsibilities that might be given to children, any five from the following list would be most appropriate for our purposes in this chapter:

Freedoms	Responsibilities
1. to read freely	to record and share
2. to get drinks and use the lavatory	to be quiet when doing so
3. to get materials and work independently	to work quietly so others can work
4. to ask questions and ask for help	to think before asking
5. to hold group discussions	to talk softly
6. to express their ideas	to listen while others express their ideas
7. to sit and work in groups	to cooperate with others

A.   1-5 Select any five from the following list:

freedom of movement for children
use of learning centers
pupil-teacher planning
individualization of instruction
flexibility of scheduling
open ended learning opportunities

6-10 Select any five from the following:

Freedoms	Responsibilities
to read freely	to record and share
to get drinks and use the lavatory	to be quiet when doing so
to get materials and work independently	to work quietly so others can work
to ask questions and ask for help	to think before asking
to hold group discussions	to talk softly
to express their ideas	to listen while others express their ideas
to sit and work in groups	to cooperate with others

B.   Assign 10 points each. If you do not achieve a score of at least 90%, you may want to re-read portions of the chapter.

A. The following are principles of learning which should be
used in work with elementary school children. A brief
description is also provided for comparison with your work.

1. <u>Motivation</u> - This principle indicates that learning
will be enhanced when you get the learner interested
in what you want him/her to learn.

2. <u>Association</u> - This principle indicates that learning
will be enhanced when you help children relate what
they are learning in school with the outside world.

3. <u>Effect</u> - This principle indicates that learning will
be enhanced when you praise pupil responses.

4. <u>Multiple Stimuli</u> - This principle indicates that
learning will be enhanced when you use films, filmstrips, movies, cassettes, maps, and other audio-
visual aids.

5. <u>Transfer</u> - This principle indicates that learning will
be enhanced when you help children transfer what they
learn in one subject area to another subject area.

6. <u>Pupil-participation</u> - This principle indicates that
learning will be enhanced when you allow pupils to
participate in learning activities.

7. <u>Individual differences</u> - This principle indicates that
learning will be enhanced when you pay attention to
individual differences.

8. <u>Evaluation</u> - This principle indicates that learning
will be enhanced when you evaluate in a manner consistent with your stated objectives.

B. The following is a list of techniques which might be used
to motivate elementary school children. You should have
been able to identify at least two:

1. fear . . . used far too much
2. curiosity
3. building upon previous experience
4. goal setting

C.   Factors you might want to consider are:

1.   Have I evaluated children in a manner consistent with the objectives I have formulated for their instructional program?

2.   Have I explained the evaluation procedure I am using to the children so they will find the grade or evaluation meaningful?

Appendix F
Evaluation KEY
Chapter 3

A. 1-5 You should include any five of the following in any order:

   motivation
   association
   effect
   multiple stimuli
   transfer
   pupil participation
   individual differences
   evaluation

   6. Motivation

   7-9 You should include any three of the following in any order:

   fear
   curiosity
   goal setting
   building upon previous experience

   10. Effect

B. Assign 10 points to each correct response. If you do not receive a score of at least 90%, you may want to re-read portions of the chapter.

131

A. You should have listed any three of the following word
    recognition skills in any order:

    1. sight vocabulary
    2. verbal context clues
    3. picture clues
    4. phonetic analysis
    5. structural analysis

B. You should have listed any four of the following compre-
    hension skills in any order:

    1. reading to find the main idea
    2. reading to select significant details
    3. reading to follow directions
    4. reading to answer questions
    5. reading to summarize and organize
    6. reading to arrive at generalizations
    7. reading to predict outcomes
    8. reading to evaluate critically
    9. reading to get meaning from phrases, sentences, and
        longer selections

C. The answer is (c)

D. The answer is (a)

E. The answer is (c)

A. 1-4 You should have listed the following four word
         recognition skills in any order:

         sight vocabulary
         context clues
         phonetic analysis
         structural analysis

    5-10 You should have listed any six of the following
         comprehension skills in any order:

         reading to find the main idea
         reading to select significant details
         reading to follow directions
         reading to answer questions
         reading to summarize and organize
         reading to arrive at generalizations
         reading to predict outcomes
         reading to evaluate critically
         reading to get meaning from phrases, sentences, and
         longer selections

    11. The answer is (a)

    12. The answer is (a)

    13. The answer is (a)

    14. The answer is (b)

    15. The answer is (d)

    16. The answer is (c)

    17. The answer is (c)

    18. The answer is (d)

    19. The answer is (c)

    20. The answer is (c)

B. Assign 5 points to each correct response. If you do not
    achieve a score of at least 90%, you may want to re-read
    portions of the chapter.

A. You should have identified one advantage of the basal reader approach that is similar to any one of the following:

   1. The stories can provide a common center of interest with a group of children.

   2. The skills program is carefully structured, systematic, and sequential.

   3. Teacher's guides are usually well organized and can save much teacher planning time.

B. The answer to this question is that there is no one best approach to reading instruction in the elementary school classroom.

C. The answer is (false).

D. Your answer should be something similar to the following:

It has been described as a scientific method of studying language.

E. Your answer should include one disadvantage that is similar to one of the following:

   1. The approach often makes it difficult for the teacher to evaluate and keep records.

   2. Skill teaching is often done in a haphazard manner.

   3. A large selection of books is needed.

F. Language experience approach.

A.   1-5 You should have listed the following five approaches
to reading instruction in any order:

Basal Reader Approach
Phonics Approach
Linguistic Approach
Individualized Approach
Language Experience Approach

6. The answer is (true).

7. The answer if (false).

8. The answer if (false).

9. The answer is (true).

10. The answer is (true).

B.   Assign 10 points to each correct response. If you do not
receive a score of at least 90%, you may want to re-read
portions of the chapter.

A.   The behavioral objective is as follows:

Children will be able to spell the word "cat" correctly.

B.   The parts of a lesson plan should be listed in the following order:

1.   Objectives
2.   Materials
3.   Introduction and Motivation
4.   Procedure
5.   Evaluation

A. Checklist for evaluation of your lesson plan

Directions: Re-read your lesson plan carefully to see that
the following criteria were met. Circle yes or no for each
item on this checklist as you examine your plan.

CHECK LIST:

CRITERIA

1. Does your plan include objectives, materials,
   introduction and motivation, procedure and
   evaluation?   YES   NO

2. Do your objectives specify the exact behavior
   you expect to observe?   YES   NO

3. Have you identified specific materials by
   titles and or page numbers?   YES   NO

4. Does your introduction and motivation
   reflect the use of a specific motivational
   technique such as fear, curiosity, building
   on previous experience, or goal setting?   YES   NO

5. Is there consistency between your stated
   objectives and your evaluation, i.e., does
   your planned evaluation include evaluation
   of all of your stated objectives?   YES   NO

B. Assign 20 points for each response in the yes column. If
   you do not receive a score of at least 80%, you may want to
   re-read portions of the chapter.

A. The following are elements of classroom management. You may have them listed in any order.

1. Classroom climate
2. Classroom control
3. Classroom discipline

B. Ideally, the open classroom teacher should strive to develop self-discipline in the children.

C. When a child becomes "irate" in class, don't pick on him/her. Separate him/her from the class and proceed until he/she "cools off."

A. 1-5 You should have listed any five of the following
         guidelines for classroom management in any order:

    *Project enthusiasm in your teaching.
    *Project security as you work with children.
    *Establish guidelines for the class.
    *Demonstrate fairness to the class in all you do.
    *Provide for individual differences.
    *Study and reflect upon the "typical characteristics
        of children at the grade level of which you are
        teaching.
    *Apply the principles of learning.
    *Identify leaders in the class and allow them to help
        keep at the task at hand.
    *Make a "When all is said and done" bulletin board.
    *Plan your lessons so you don't leave gaps in your
        teaching.
    *Organize materials and equipment.

    6-10 You should have listed any five of the following
         guidelines for classroom discipline in any order:

    *When you face a discipline problem, solve it then
        within the framework of the guidelines that you
        have established.
    *Handle your own "discipline problems" when at all
        possible.
    *When a child becomes "irate" don't pick on him/her.
    *Don't try to become a "buddy" to children.
    *Be friendly but firm with all children, both in and
        out of the classroom.
    *Don't play favorites in class.
    *Don't make up last minute "punishments."
    *Don't fight aggression with aggression.
    *Vary the tone of your voice and the rate at which you
        speak to hold interest.
    *Study permanent records for clues to reasons for
        problem behavior.
    *Remember, you were once a child.

B. Assign 10 points to each correct response. If you do not
    achieve a score of at least 90%, you may want to re-read
    portions of the chapter.

147

A. You should have listed the following five elements of the
    language arts program in any order:

    1. spelling
    2. handwriting
    3. listening
    4. speaking
    5. written composition

B. Any five activities that require children to use spelling,
    handwriting, listening, speaking, or written composition
    during a reading activity.

C. Your description should be similar to the following:

    In general, a learning station consists of a group of
    children working together at a well-defined task. The task
    can easily involve the integration of several areas of
    reading and other language arts as children work on such
    things as social studies and science projects.

D. The basis of all language skills development is the devel-
    opment of oral language.

A. 1. The answer is (true).

    2. The answer is (false).

    3. The answer is (false).

    4. The answer is (false).

    5. The answer is (false).

    6 - 10   You should have included any five of the
              following in any order:

              *Have children listen to stories to determine
                  important ideas or sequence.
              *Have children use their speaking skills to tell
                  about what they have read.
              *Have children use letter writing skills as they
                  write reactions to what they have read.
              *Have children write their reactions to what they
                  have read.
              *Have upper grade children orally debate issues
                  related to what they have read.
              *Utilize learning stations.
              *Utilize a variety of game activities such as
                  Dictionary, Golden Treasury Box, Lively
                  Word, Sentence Bag, or Story Box.
              *Have children use speaking skills to discuss
                  unusual uses of words found in stories.
              *Have children orally discuss specific sentence
                  structure found in stories.

B. Assign 10 points to each correct response. If you do not
    achieve a score of at least 90%, you may want to re-read
    portions of the chapter.

151

A. While there are several ways the teacher might initiate a diagnostic approach, the following might be very appropriate steps to take early in the approach:

   1. Obtain an intelligence quotient for each child. This is important information for the teacher to have since intelligence is a factor affecting reading growth. As well, the information can be used to compute reading expectancy.

   2. Compute reading expectancy. This computation will provide a grade equivalent score that can be used for comparison with reading achievement scores. Without this information, the teacher can only compare reading achievement scores with grade placement.

   3. Administer a word recognition test. Such a test is usually short and will indicate the grade level at which children can recognize words. This information will be helpful in the selection of an appropriate reading achievement test.

B. One such test would be the Peabody Picture Vocabulary Test. Another example would be the Slosson Intelligence Test for Children and Adults.

C. The Informal Reading Inventory could be used to determine the instructional, frustration, and independent reading levels.

A. The following are the steps and the order in which they
    should be followed as you initiate a diagnostic approach to
    reading instruction:

        1.   Obtain an intelligence quotient
        2.   Compute reading expectancy
        3.   Administer a word recognition test
        4.   Administer a reading achievement test

    The following are two tests that could be used by the
    classroom teacher to determine the approximate intelligence
    quotient:

        5.   Peabody Picture Vocabulary Test
        6.   Slosson Intelligence Test for Children and Adults

    The following reading levels can be obtained from the
    Informal Reading Inventory:

        7.   Instructional
        8.   Independent
        9.   Frustration
       10.   Classroom Reading Inventory by Silvaroli

B. Assign 10 points each. If you do not achieve a score of at
    least 90%, you may want to re-read portions of the chapter.

A. The following are guidelines that should be followed.
    Check to see that you have three that are close to those in
    the following list:

    1.   Attack only one or two deficiencies at a time.
    2.   Let the children observe you reading so you become a
         good model.
    3.   Use an interest inventory and build on children's
         interests.
    4.   Be sure that corrective work involves instructional,
         independent, and recreational reading activities.
    5.   Use easy material to start so you can insure pupil
         success.
    6.   Work to overcome children's feelings of defeat and
         inadequacy.
    7.   Provide short periods of practice.
    8.   Keep an open mind toward various approaches and
         materials since no one approach or material can
         guarantee results.
    9.   Take suggestions of children into account as a program
         is developed.
    10. Diagnosis should be continuous and adjustments should
         be made as the program develops.

B. The following are elements of the classroom environment
    important for the support of corrective reading activities.
    Your answer should include responses that are close to five
    of the following:

    1.   The room should include a library or reading corner.
    2.   The reading area should be comfortable.
    3.   The teacher should be able to be heard by the chil-
         dren.
    4.   Group instruction should be given in such a way that
         other children are not disturbed.
    5.   Pupils' language arts work should be displayed.
    6.   Charts should be posted to help guide reading, listen-
         ing, and speaking skill development.
    7.   The room should contain a variety of books.
    8.   The room should provide a place for book reviews and
         children's comments.
    9.   The room should contain charts to reinforce word
         analysis skill development.
    10. The room should include a place where children can
         exchange stories they have written with other chil-
         dren.

C.   Such children need more drill on sight vocabulary. The
     teacher needs to find novel ways to stimulate interest in
     such drill.

D.   Such children might profit from drawing four pictures
     depicting four main ideas in a particular story.

A.   1-5   Select any five from the following list:

- a. Attack only one or two deficiencies at a time.
- b. Let the children observe you reading so you become a good model.
- c. Use an interest inventory and build on children's interests.
- d. Be sure that corrective work involves instructional, independent, and recreational reading activities.
- e. Use easy material to start so you can insure pupil success.
- f. Work to overcome children's feelings of defeat and inadequacy.
- g. Provide short periods of practice.
- h. Keep an open mind toward various approaches and materials since no one approach or material can guarantee results.
- i. Take suggestions of children into account as a program is developed.
- j. Diagnosis should be continuous and adjustments should be made as the program develops.

6-8   List any two from the following list:

- a. The room should include a library or reading corner.
- b. The reading area should be comfortable.
- c. The teacher should be able to be heard by the children.
- d. Group instruction should be given in such a way that other children are not disturbed.
- e. Pupils' language arts work should be displayed.
- f. Charts should be posted to help guide reading, listening, and speaking skill development.
- g. The room should contain a variety of books.
- h. The room should provide a place for book reviews and children's comments.
- i. The room should contain charts to reinforce word analysis skill development.
- j. The room should include a place where children can exchange stories they have written with other children.

9. Provide such children with a plain white card to use under lines of print while reading.

10. Give such children riddles to solve and also assign fact questions to be answered in writing.

B. Assign 10 points each. If you do not achieve a score of at least 90%, you may want to re-read portions of the chapter.

"YOUR OWN PAPER"

(Answer Blanks)

A.   What is reading?

_____

_____

_____

_____

B.   Reading Skills:

_____

_____

_____

_____

C.   Factors which affect reading growth:

_____

_____

_____

_____

D.   The difference between instructional
     independent reading:

_____

_____

_____

_____

E.   Reminder - The answer KEY for this activity
     can be found on page 117 of the appendices.

A.

    1. _____

    2. _____

    3. _____

    4. _____

    5. _____

    6. _____

    7. _____

    8. _____

    9. _____

   10. _____

B.   Reminder - The answer KEY for this activity can be found on page 121 of the appendices.

"Your Own Paper"
Pre-assessment Answer Blank
Chapter 2

A. Characteristics of "open" or
    democratic" informal learning
    environment:

    1. _____

    2. _____

    3. _____

    4. _____

    5. _____

B. Freedoms and Responsibilities to be
    given to children in the classroom:

    Freedoms   Responsibilities

    1. _____

    2. _____

    3. _____

    4. _____

    5. _____

C. Reminder - The answer KEY for this
    activity can be found on page 123 of
    the appendices.

A.

    1. _____

    2. _____

    3. _____

    4. _____

    5. _____

    6. _____

    7. _____

    8. _____

    9. _____

  10. _____

B.   Reminder - The answer KEY for this activity can be found on page 125 of the appendices.

A. The following are some principles of
    learning:

_____

_____

_____

_____

_____

_____

B. Ways to motivate children:

_____

_____

_____

_____

_____

_____

C. Factors to consider if you were going
    to evaluate children in reading:

_____

_____

D. Reminder - The answer KEY for this
    activity can be found on page 127 of
    the appendices.

A.

    1. _____

    2. _____

    3. _____

    4. _____

    5. _____

    6. _____

    7. _____

    8. _____

    9. _____

   10. _____

B.   Reminder - The answer KEY for this activity can be found on page 131 of the appendices.

177

A.   Word recognition skills that can be
used to unlock unfamiliar words:

_____

_____

_____

B.   Specific comprehension skills that are
needed by the effective reader:

_____

_____

_____

_____

C.   The following is not a consonant blend:

_____

D.   The following word contains a
diphthong:

_____

E.   The following word contains an open
syllable:

_____

F.   Reminder: The answer KEY for this
activity can be found on page 133 of
the appendices.

A.

_____

1. _____

2. _____

3. _____

4. _____

5. _____

6. _____

7. _____

8. _____

9. _____

10. _____

B. Reminder – The answer KEY for this activity can be found on page 135 of the appendices.

"Your Own Paper"
Pre-assessment Answer Blank
<u>Chapter 5</u>

A. The following is one advantage of the
    Basal Reader Approach to reading
    instruction:

    _____

    _____

B. The following is my answer regarding
    the best approach to reading
    instruction:

    _____

    _____

C. _____

D. The following is a description of
    the term "linguistics:"

    _____

    _____

    _____

    _____

    _____

E. Reminder – The answer KEY for this
    activity can be found on page 137 of
    the appendices.

"Your Own Paper"
Evaluation Answer Blank
<u>Chapter 5</u>

A. _____

    1. _____

    2. _____

    3. _____

    4. _____

    5. _____

    6. _____

    7. _____

    8. _____

    9. _____

  10. _____

B.   Reminder - The answer KEY for this activity can be found on page 139 of the appendices.

A. The following is a behavioral
    objective:

    _____

    _____

B. The following are the parts of a lesson
    plan:

    _____

    1. _____

    2. _____

    3. _____

    4. _____

    5. _____

C. Reminder – The answer KEY for this
    activity can be found on page 141
    of the appendices.

187

"Your Own Paper"
Evaluation Answer Blank
Chapter 6

A.   My lesson Plan (tear out pages 189 and
     191 for this activity).

     Name of book _____

     Title of story _____

     Pages _____

(continued on next page)

(My lesson plan continued)

B. Reminder – The answer KEY for this
    activity can be found on page 143
    of the appendices.

"Your Own Paper"
Pre-assessment Answer Blank
<u>Chapter 7</u>

A. Three elements of classroom management:

_____

_____

_____

B. The kind of discipline the teacher
    should develop:

_____

_____

_____

_____

_____

C. What to do with the "angered" or
    "irate" child:

_____

_____

_____

_____

_____

D. Reminder - The answer KEY for this
    activity can be found on page of 145 of
    the appendices.

"Your Own Paper"
Evaluation Answer Blank
<u>Chapter 7</u>

A.

1. _____

2. _____

3. _____

4. _____

5. _____

6. _____

7. _____

8. _____

9. _____

10. _____

B.   Reminder - The answer KEY for this
     activity can be found on page 147 of
     the appendices.

A. Five "elements" of the total language
    arts program:

    _____

    1. _____

    2. _____

    3. _____

    4. _____

    5. _____

B. Five activities that can be used to
    integrate reading with other areas of
    language arts:

    _____

    1. _____

    2. _____

    3. _____

    4. _____

    5. _____

C. My brief description of a learning
    station:

    _____

    _____

    _____

    _____

D. The following is the foundation of all
    language skill development:

    _____

E. Reminder: The answer KEY for this
    activity can be found on page 149 of
    the appendices.

197

"Your Own Paper"
Evaluation Answer Blank
Chapter 8

A.

_____

1. _____

2. _____

3. _____

4. _____

5. _____

6. _____

7. _____

8. _____

9. _____

10. _____

B.   Reminder – The answer KEY for this
     activity can be found on page 151 of
     the appendices.

"Your Own Paper"
Pre-assessment Answer Blank
<u>Chapter 9</u>

A.   The first 3 steps in a diagnostic
approach to reading instruction:

_____

1.   _____

2.   _____

3.   _____

B.   The following is the name of one test
that could be used to determine the
intelligence quotient of a child:

_____

C.   The following is the name of a test
that could be used to determine the
instructional, frustration, and
independent reading levels of a child:

_____

D.   Reminder - The answer KEY for this
activity can be found on page 153 of
the appendices.

"Your Own Paper"
Evaluation Answer Blank
<u>Chapter 9</u>

A.

_____

1. _____

2. _____

3. _____

4. _____

5. _____

6. _____

7. _____

8. _____

9. _____

10. _____

B.   Reminder – The answer KEY for this
      activity can be found on page 155 of
      the appendices.

A.   Guidelines to be followed:

_____

1.   _____

2.   _____

3.   _____

_____

B.   Elements of classroom environment that
     will support correction:

1.   _____

2.   _____

3.   _____

4.   _____

5.   _____

C.   Corrective activity for sight
     vocabulary:

_____

_____

_____

D.   Corrective activity for main ideas:

_____

_____

_____

E.   Reminder - The answer KEY for this
     activity can be found on page 157 of
     the appendices.

A.

_____

1. _____

2. _____

3. _____

4. _____

5. _____

6. _____

7. _____

8. _____

9. _____

_____

_____

10. _____

_____

_____

B. Reminder – The answer KEY for this
activity can be found on page 161 of
the appendices.

207

REFERENCES

Bader, Lois, A. <u>Reading Diagnosis and Remediation in Classroom and Clinic</u>, New York: Macmillan Publishing Co. Inc., 1980.

Bond, Guy, L., Tinker, Miles, A. Wasson, Barbara, B., <u>Reading Difficulties: Their Diagnosis and Correction</u>, Englewood Cliffs, New Jersey: Prentice-Hall, Inc., 1979.

Burns, P.C. <u>The Language Arts in Childhood Education</u>, Chicago: Rand McNally and Company, 1966.

Carrillo, L.W. <u>Teaching Reading-A Handbook</u>, New York: St. Martin's Press, 1976.

Dallmann, M., Rouch, R., Chang, L., and DeBoer, J. <u>The Teaching of Reading</u>, (Fourth Edition), New York: Holt, Reinhart, and Winston, Inc., 1974.

Dechant, E.V. <u>Improving The Teaching of Reading</u>, Englewood Cliffs, New Jersey: Prentice-Hall, Inc., 1974.

Guenther, A.R. "What is This Open Education?" <u>Pennsylvania School Journal</u>, April 1972, p. 165.

Harris, A.J., and Sipay, E.R. <u>How To Increase Reading Ability</u>, (Sixth Edition), New York: David McKay Co., Inc., 1975.

Heilman, A.W. <u>Phonics in Proper Perspective</u>, (Third Edition), Columbus, Ohio: Charles E. Merrill Publishing Co., 1976.

Hurt, Thomas, Scott, Michael, D., McCroskey, James, C. <u>Communication in The Classroom</u>, Reading, Massachusetts: Addison-Wesley Publishing Company, 1978.

Johnson, L.W., Bany, M.A. <u>Classroom Management</u>, London: The Macmillan Company, 1970.

Karlin, R. <u>Teaching Elementary School Reading</u>, New York: Harcourt Brace Jovanovich, Inc., 1975.

Miller, W.H. <u>The First R-Elementary Reading Today</u>, New York: Holt, Rinehart and Winston, 1977.

Putt, Robert C. <u>Working With The Student Teacher</u>, Dansville, New York: Instructor Publications, 1971.

Tiedt, I.M., and Tiedt, S.W. Comparative English In The
    Elementary School, Englewood Cliffs, New Jersey: Prentice-
    Hall, 1967.

Wilson, R.M., and Hall, M. Reading and the Elementary School
    Child, New York: Van Nostrand Reinhold Company, 1972.

Zintz, Miles, V. Corrective Reading, Dubuque, Iowa: Wm. C.
    Brown Company Publishers, 1981.

About the Author

Robert C. Putt is currently an Associate Professor in the Department of Education, Mansfield University, Mansfield, Pennsylvania. He teaches undergraduate and graduate reading courses at the University and has served as Director of the Reading and Study Clinic for the past eight years. His twenty-three years of teaching experience have also included elementary classroom teaching, supervision of student teachers, college methods course instruction, teaching of reading at the elementary and secondary level, service as a reading consultant, and Assistant and Acting Chairperson at the University. He has published numerous articles in professional journals, and is author of the handbook Working With The Student Teacher. Dr. Putt received his B.S. in Elementary Education from S.U.N.Y. at Geneseo in 1960, the M.S. in Education with a specialty in reading from S.U.N.Y. Fredonia in 1965, and the D.Ed. in Curriculum and Instruction from the Pennsylvania State University in 1977.